HUNGER

KNUT HAMSUN was born of peasant stock in central Norway, in 1859. He started work at an early age, and led a jack-of-all-trades existence. In the 1880s he spent two periods in America. His first novel was *Hunger* (1890). Hamsun rejected the social preoccupations of contemporary fiction, and criticised its lack of understanding of 'the unconscious life of the mind'. His novel *Mysteries* (1892) was intended as a demonstration of what the new literature should be. The best known of Hamsun's other novels are *Pan* (1894) and *Victoria* (1898). Hamsun died in 1952, and since then a growing body of readers has been drawn to his work by its extraordinary qualities of insight and imagination.

SVERRE LYNGSTAD, Distinguished Professor Emeritus of English at the New Jersey Institute of Technology, is the author of many books and articles on Scandinavian literature, including *Sigurd Hoel's Fiction* (1984) and *Knut Hamsun, Novelist: A Critical Assessment* (2005). Among his translations from Norwegian are Sigurd Hoel's *Meeting at the Milestone* (2002) and a number of Knut Hamsun's novels, most recently *Victoria* (2005). Dr Lyngstad has received several awards and honours, including the St Olav Medal and the Knight's Cross, First Class, of the Royal Norwegian Order of Merit.

HUNGER

Knut Hamsun

Translated by Sverre Lyngstad

CANONGATE
Edinburgh · London · New York · Melbourne

First published in Great Britain in 1996 by Canongate Books Ltd,
14 High Street, Edinburgh, EH1 1TE

'The Art of Hunger' by Paul Auster first published in 1970 in
the United States of America by Farrar, Straus and Giroux

This edition first published by Canongate Books in 2006

4

Introduction essay 'The Art of Hunger' by Paul Auster
reprinted with the kind permission of Faber and Faber

The publisher gratefully acknowledges subsidy from the
Scottish Arts Council towards the publication of this volume

British Library Cataloguing-in-Publication Data
A catalogue record for this book is available on
request from the British Library

1 84195 819 0 (10-digit ISBN)
978 1 84195 819 4 (13-digit ISBN)

Typeset by Palimpsest Book Production Ltd,
Grangemouth, Stirlingshire

Printed and bound in Great Britain by
Clays Ltd, St Ives plc

www.meetatthegate.com

Contents

Introduction

THE ART OF HUNGER

What is important, it seems to me, is not so much to defend a culture whose existence has never kept a man from going hungry, as to extract, from what is called culture, ideas whose compelling force is identical with that of hunger.

—Antonin Artaud

A young man comes to a city. He has no name, no home, no work: he has come to the city to write. He writes. Or, more exactly, he does not write. He starves to the point of death.

The city is Christiania (Oslo); the year is 1890. The young man wanders through the streets: the city is a labyrinth of hunger, and all his days are the same. He writes unsolicited articles for a local paper. He worries about his rent, his disintegrating clothes, the difficulty of finding his next meal. He suffers. He nearly goes mad. He is never more than one step from collapse.

Still, he writes. Now and then he manages to sell an article, to find a temporary reprieve from his misery. But he is too weak to write steadily and can rarely finish the pieces he has begun. Among his abortive works are an essay entitled 'Crimes of the Future,' a philosophical tract on the freedom of the will, an allegory about a bookstore fire (the books are brains), and a play set in the Middle Ages, *The Sign of the Cross*. The process is inescapable: he must eat in order to write. But if he does not write, he will not eat. And if he cannot eat, he cannot write. He cannot write.

He writes. He does not write. He wanders through the streets of the city. He talks to himself in public. He frightens people away from him. When, by chance, he comes into some money, he gives it away. He is evicted from his room. He eats, and then throws everything up. At one point, he has a brief flirtation with a girl, but nothing comes of it except humiliation. He hungers. He curses the world. He does not die. In the end, for no apparent reason, he signs on board a ship and leaves the city.

These are the bare bones of Knut Hamsun's first novel, *Hunger*. It is a work devoid of plot, action, and – but for the narrator-character. By nineteenth-century standards, it is a work in which nothing happens. The radical subjectivity of the narrator effectively eliminates the basic concerns of the traditional novel. Similar to the hero's plan to make an 'invisible detour' when he came to the problem of space and time in one of his essays, Hamsun manages to dispense with historical time, the basic organizing principle of nineteenth-century fiction. He gives us an account only of the hero's worst struggles with hunger. Other, less difficult times, in which his hunger has been appeased – even though they might last as long as a week – are passed off in one or two sentences. Historical time is obliterated in favor of inner duration. With only an arbitrary beginning and an arbitrary ending, the novel faithfully records the vagaries of the narrator's mind, following each thought from its mysterious inception through all its meanderings, until it dissipates and the next thought begins. What happens is allowed to happen.

This novel cannot even claim to have a redeeming social value. Although *Hunger* puts us in the jaws of misery, it offers no analysis of that misery, contains no call to political action. Hamsun, who turned fascist in his old age during the Second World War, never concerned himself with the problems of class injustice, and his narrator – hero, like Dostoevsky's Raskolnikov, is not so much an underdog as a monster of intellectual arrogance. Pity plays no part in *Hunger*. The hero suffers, but only because he has chosen to suffer. Hamsun's art is such that he rigorously prevents us from feeling any compassion for his character. From the very beginning, it is made clear that the hero need not starve. Solutions exist, if not in the city, then at least in departure. But buoyed by an obsessive, suicidal pride, the young man's actions continually betray a scorn for his own best interests.

I began running so as to punish myself, left street after street behind me, pushed myself on with inward jeers, and screeched silently and furiously at myself whenever I felt like stopping. With the help of these exertions I ended up far along Pile Street. When I finally did stop, almost weeping with anger that I couldn't run any farther, my whole body trembled, and I threw myself down on a house stoop. 'Not so fast!' I said. And to torture myself right, I stood up again and forced myself to stand there, laughing at myself and gloating over my own fatigue. Finally, after a few minutes I nodded and so gave myself permission to sit down; however, I chose the most uncomfortable spot on the stoop.

He seeks out what is most difficult in himself, courting pain and adversity in the same way other men seek out pleasure. He goes hungry, not because he has to, but from some inner compulsion, as if to wage a hunger strike against himself. Before the book begins, before the reader has been made the privileged witness of his fate, the hero's course of action has been fixed. A process is already in motion, and although the hero cannot control it, that does not mean he is unaware of what he is doing.

> I was conscious all the time that I was following mad whims without being able to do anything about it ... Despite my alienation from myself at that moment, and even though I was nothing but a battleground for invisible forces, I was aware of every detail of what was going on around me.

Having withdrawn into a nearly perfect solitude, he has become both the subject and object of his own experiment. Hunger is the means by which this split takes place, the catalyst, so to speak, of altered consciousness.

> I had noticed very clearly that every time I went hungry a little too long it was as though my brains simply ran quietly out of my head and left me empty. My head became light and floating, I could no longer feel its weight on my shoulders ..

If it is an experiment, however, it has nothing to do with the scientific method. There are no controls, no stable points of reference – only variables. Nor can this separation of mind and body be reduced to a philosophical abstraction. We are not in the realm of ideas here. It is a physical state, brought into being under conditions of extreme duress. Mind and body have been weakened; the hero has lost control over both his thought and actions. And yet he persists in trying to control his destiny. This is the paradox, the game of circular logic that is played out through the pages of the book. It is an impossible situation for the hero. For he has willfully brought himself to the brink of danger. To give up starving would not mean victory, it would simply mean that the game was over. He wants to survive, but only on his own terms: survival that will bring him face to face with death.

He fasts. But not in the way a Christian would fast. He is not denying earthly life in anticipation of heavenly life; he is simply refusing to live the life he has been given. And the longer he goes on with his fast, the more death intrudes itself upon his life. He approaches death, creeps toward the edge of the abyss, and once there, clings to it, unable to move either forward or backward. Hunger, which opens the void, does not have the power to seal it up. A brief moment of Pascalian terror has been transformed into a permanent condition.

His fast, then, is a contradiction. To persist in it would mean death, and with death the fast would end. He must therefore stay alive, but only to the extent that it keeps him on the point of death. The idea of ending is resisted in the interests of maintaining the constant possibility of the end. Because his fasting neither posits a goal nor offers a promise of redemption, its contradiction must remain unresolved. As such, it is an image of despair, generated by the same self-consuming passion as the sickness unto death. The soul, in its despair, seeks to devour itself, and because it cannot – precisely because it despairs – sinks further into despair.

Unlike a religious art, in which self-debasement can play an ultimately cleansing role (the meditative poetry of the seventeenth century, for example), hunger only simulates the dialectic of salvation. In Fulke Greville's poem, 'Down in the depth of mine iniquity,' the poet is able to look into a 'fatal mirror of transgression' which 'shows man as fruit of his degeneration,' but he knows that this is only the first step in a two-fold process, for it is in this mirror that Christ is revealed 'for the same sins dying / And from that hell I feared, to free me, come . . .' In Hamsun's novel, however, once the depths have been sounded, the mirror of meditation remains empty.

He remains at the bottom, and no God will come to rescue the young man. He cannot even depend on the props of social convention to keep him standing. He is rootless, without friends, denuded of objects. Order has disappeared for him; everything has become random. His actions are inspired by nothing but whim and ungovernable urge, the weary frustration of anarchic discontent. He pawns his waistcoat in order to give alms to a beggar, hires a carriage in search of a fictitious acquaintance, knocks on strangers' doors, and repeatedly asks the time of passing policemen, for the single reason that he fancies to do so. He does not revel in these actions, however. They remain profoundly disquieting for him. Furiously trying to stabilize his life, to put an end to his wanderings, find a room, and settle down to his writing, he is thwarted by the fast he has set in motion. Once it starts, hunger does not release its progenitor-victim until its lesson has been made unforgettable. The hero is seized against his will by a force of his own making and is compelled to respond to its demands.

He loses everything – even himself. Reach the bottom of a Godless hell, and identity disappears. It is no accident that Hamsun's hero has no name: as time goes on, he is truly shorn of his self. What names he chooses to give himself are all inventions, summoned forth on the spur of the moment. He cannot say who he is because he does not know. His name is a lie, and with this lie the reality of his world vanishes.

He peers into the darkness hunger has created for him, and what he finds is a void of language. Reality has become a confusion of thingless names and nameless things for him. The connection between self and world has been broken.

I remained a while looking into the dark – this dense substance of darkness that had no bottom, which I couldn't understand. My thoughts could not grasp such a thing. It seemed to be dark

beyond all measurement, and I felt its presence weigh me down.
I closed my eyes and took to singing half aloud and rocking
myself back and forth on the cot to amuse myself, but it did
no good. The dark had captured my brain and gave me not
an instant of peace. What if I myself became dissolved into the
dark, turned into it?

At the precise moment that he is in the greatest fear of losing
possession of himself, he suddenly imagines that he has invented
a new word: *Kuboaa* – a word in no language, a word with no
meaning.

I had arrived at the joyful insanity hunger was: I was empty and
free of pain, and my thoughts no longer had any check.

He tries to think of a meaning for his word but can only come
up with what it doesn't mean, which is neither *God,* nor the
Tivoli Gardens, nor *cattle show*, nor *padlock*, nor *sunrise*, nor
emigration, nor *tobacco factory*, nor *yarn*.

No, the word was actually intended to mean something spiritual,
a feeling, a state of mind – if I could only understand it? And I
thought and thought to find something spiritual.

But he does not succeed. Voices, not his own, begin to intrude,
to confuse him, and he sinks deeper into chaos. After a violent fit,
in which he imagines himself to be dying, all goes still, with no
sounds but those of his own voice, rolling back from the walls.
   This episode is perhaps the most painful in the book. But
it is only one of many examples of the hero's language dis-
ease. Throughout the narrative, his pranks most often take
the form of lies. Retrieving his lost pencil from a pawnshop
(he had accidentally left it in the pocket of a vest he had

sold), he tells the proprietor that it was with this very pencil that he had written his three-volume treatise on Philosophical Consciousness. An insignificant pencil, he admits, but he has a sentimental attachment to it. To an old man on a park bench he recites the fantastic story of a Mr Happolati, the inventor of the electric prayer book. Asking a store clerk to wrap his last possession, a tattered green blanket that he is too ashamed to carry around exposed to view, he explains that it is not really the blanket he wants wrapped, but the pair of priceless vases he has folded inside the blanket. Not even the girl he courts is immune from this sort of fiction. He invents a name for her, a name that pleases him for its beauty, and he refuses to call her by anything else.

These lies have a meaning beyond the jests of the moment. In the realm of language the lie has the same relationship to truth that evil has to good in the realm of morals. That is the convention, and it works if we believe in it. But Hamsun's hero no longer believes in anything. Lies and truths are as one to him. Hunger has led him into the darkness, and there is no turning back.

This equation of language and morals becomes the gist of the final episode in *Hunger*.

My brain grew clearer, I understood that I was close to total collapse. I put my hands against the wall and shoved to push myself away from it. The street was still dancing around. I began to hiccup from fury, and struggled with every bit of energy against my collapse, fought a really stout battle not to fall down. I didn't want to fall, I wanted to die standing. A wholesale grocer's cart came by, and I saw it was filled with potatoes, but out of fury, from sheer obstinacy, I decided that they were not potatoes at all, they were cabbages, and I swore violent oaths that they were cabbages. I heard my own words very well, and I took the oath again and again on this lie, and swore deliberately just to have the delightful satisfaction of committing such clear perjury. I became drunk over this superb sin, I lifted three fingers in the air and swore with trembling lips in the name of the Father, the Son, and the Holy Ghost that they were cabbages.

And that is the end of it. There are only two possibilities left for the hero now: live or die; and he chooses to live. He has said no to society, no to God, no to his own words. Later that same day, he leaves the city. There is no longer any need to continue the fast. Its work has been done.

Hunger: or a portrait of the artist as a young man. But it is an apprenticeship that has little in common with the early struggles of other writers. Hamsun's hero is no Stephen Dedalus, and there is hardly a word in *Hunger* about aesthetic theory. The world of art has been translated into the world of the body – and the original text has been abandoned. Hunger is not a metaphor; it is the very crux of the problem itself. If others, such as Rimbaud, with his program for the voluntary derangement of the senses, have turned the body into an aesthetic principle in its own right, Hamsun's hero steadfastly rejects the opportunity to use his deficiencies to his own advantage. He is weak, he has lost control over his thoughts, and yet he continues to strive for lucidity in his writing. But hunger affects his prose in the same way it affects his life. Although he is willing to sacrifice everything for his art, even submit to the worst forms of debasement and misery, all he has really done is make it impossible for himself to write. You cannot write on an empty stomach, no matter how hard you try. But it would be wrong to dismiss the hero of *Hunger* as a fool or a madman. In spite of the evidence, he knows what he is doing. He does not want to succeed. He wants to fail.

Something new is happening here, some new thought about the nature of art is being proposed in *Hunger*. It is first of all an art that is indistinguishable from the life of the artist who makes it. That is not to say an art of autobiographical excess, but rather, an art that is the direct expression of the effort to express itself. In other words, an art of hunger: an art of need, of necessity, of desire. Certainty yields to doubt, form gives way to process. There can be no arbitrary imposition of order, and yet, more than ever, there is the obligation to achieve clarity. It is an art that begins with the knowledge that there are no right answers. For that reason, it becomes essential to ask the right questions. One finds them by living them. To quote Samuel Beckett:

> What I am saying does not mean that there will henceforth be no form in art. It only means that there will be a new form, and that this form will be of such a type that it admits the chaos and does not try to say that the chaos is really something else . . To find a form that accommodates the mess, that is the task of the artist now.*

Hamsun gives the portrait of this artist in the first stages of his development. But it is in Kafka's story, *A Hunger Artist,* that the aesthetics of hunger receives its most meticulous elaboration. Here the contradictions of the fast conducted by Hamsun's hero – and the artistic impasse it leads to – are joined in a parable that deals with an artist whose art consists in fasting. The hunger artist is at once an artist and not an artist. Though he wants his performances to be admired, he insists that they shouldn't be admired, because they have nothing to do with art. He has chosen to fast only because he could never find any food that

---

* From an interview with Tom Driver, 'Beckett at the Madeleine,' in *The Columbia University Forum*, Summer 1961.

he liked. His performances are therefore not spectacles for the amusement of others, but the unravelling of a private despair that he has permitted others to watch.

Like Hamsun's hero, the hunger artist has lost control over himself. Beyond the theatrical device of sitting in his cage, his art in no way differs from his life, even what his life would have been had he not become a performer. He is not trying to please anyone. In fact, his performances cannot even be understood or appreciated.

> No one could possibly watch the hunger artist continuously, day and night, and so no one could produce firsthand evidence that the fast had really been rigorous and continuous; only the artist himself could know that; he was therefore bound to be the sole completely satisfied spectator of his own fast.

This is not the classic story of the misunderstood artist, however. For the very nature of the fast resists comprehension. Knowing itself from the outset to be an impossibility, and condemning itself to certain failure, it is a process that moves asymptotically toward death, destined to reach neither fruition nor destruction. In Kafka's story, the hunger artist dies, but only because he forsakes his art, abandoning the restrictions that had been imposed on him by his manager. The hunger artist goes too far. But that is the risk, the danger inherent in any act of art: you must be willing to give your life.

In the end, the art of hunger can be described as an existential art. It is a way of looking death in the face, and by death I mean death as we live it today: without God, without hope of salvation. Death as the abrupt and absurd end of life.

I do not believe that we have come any farther than this. It is even possible that we have been here much longer than we are willing to admit. In all this time, however, only a few artists have been able to recognize it. It takes courage, and not many of us would be willing to risk everything for nothing. But that is what happens in *Hunger*, a novel written in 1890. Hamsun's character systematically unburdens himself of every belief in every system, and in the end, by means of the hunger he has inflicted upon himself, he arrives at nothing. There is nothing to keep him going – and yet he keeps on going. He walks straight into the twentieth century.

—Paul Auster, 1970

Part One

It was in those days when I wandered about hungry in Kristiania, that strange city which no one leaves before it has set its mark upon him. . . .

Lying awake in my attic room, I hear a clock strike six downstairs. It was fairly light already and people were beginning to walk up and down the stairs. Over by the door, where my room was papered with old issues of *Morgenbladet*, I could see, very clearly, a notice from the Director of Lighthouses, and just left of it a fat, swelling ad for freshly baked bread by Fabian Olsen, Baker.

As soon as I opened my eyes I started wondering, by force of habit, whether I had anything to look forward to today. I had been somewhat hard up lately; my belongings had been taken to 'Uncle' one after the other, I had grown nervous and irritable, and a couple of times I had even stayed in bed for a day or so because of dizziness. Every now and then, when I was lucky, I managed to get five kroner for an article from some newspaper or other.

As it grew lighter and lighter I started reading the ads over by the door; I could even make out the thin, grinning

3

letters concerning 'Shrouds at Madam Andersen's, main entrance to the right'. This occupied me for quite a while – I heard the clock strike eight downstairs before I rose and got dressed.

I opened the window and looked out. From where I stood I had a view of a clothesline and an open field; in the distance was a forge, left over from a burned-down black-smith's shop where some workers were busy cleaning up. I leaned forward with my elbows on the windowsill and gazed at the sky. It promised to be a clear day. Autumn had arrived, that lovely, cool time of year when everything changes colour and dies. The streets had already begun to get noisy, tempting me to go out. This empty room, where the floor rocked up and down at every step I took, was like a horrible, broken-down coffin. There was no proper lock on the door and no stove in the room; I used to sleep in my socks at night so they would dry a little before morning. The only thing I had to amuse myself with was a small red rocking chair where I used to sit in the evening, dozing and musing on all manner of things. When the wind blew hard and the doors downstairs were open, all sorts of eerie, whistling sounds floated up through the floor and out from the walls, and the *Morgenbladet* over by the door would get tears in it the length of my hand.

I stood up and searched through a bundle over in the corner by the bed for a bit of breakfast, but found nothing and went back again to the window.

God knows, I thought, if there is any point to my looking for work any more! All those refusals, those half promises and flat 'No's, hopes cherished only to be dashed, fresh attempts that always came to nothing

– all this had killed my courage. Finally I had applied for a job as a bill collector but been too late; besides I couldn't post a fifty-kroner bond. There was always something or other in the way. I also signed up for the fire brigade. There we stood, a half-hundred of us, in the entrance hall, throwing our chests out to give an impression of strength and fearlessness. A deputy chief went around inspecting these applicants, feeling their arm muscles and asking a question or two, and me he passed over, merely shaking his head and saying I was unfit because of my glasses. I showed up again, without glasses, standing there with knitted brows and making my eyes sharp as razors, but again the man passed over me, and he smiled – he must have recognised me. The worst of it was, my clothes were getting to be so shabby that I could no longer present myself for a position like a respectable person.

It had been going steadily downhill for me all along, and how! In the end, strange to say, I was stripped of every-thing under the sun, I didn't even have a comb any more or a book to read when life became too dreary. All summer long I had haunted the cemeteries and Palace Park, where I would sit and prepare articles for the newspapers, column after column about all sorts of things – strange whimsies, moods, caprices of my restless brain. In my desperation I had often chosen the most far-fetched subjects, which cost me hours and hours of effort and were never accepted. When a piece was finished I began a fresh one, and I wasn't very often discouraged by the editor's no; I kept telling myself that, some day, I was bound to succeed. And indeed, when I was lucky and it turned out well, I would occasionally get five kroner for an afternoon's work.

Getting up from the window again, I stepped over to the wash-stand and sprinkled a bit of water on the shiny knees of my trousers, to darken them and make them look newer. This done, I put paper and pencil in my pocket, as usual, and went out. I stole quietly down the stairs to avoid attracting the attention of my landlady; my rent had been due a few days ago and I had nothing to pay her with any more.

It was nine o'clock. The air was filled with voices and the rumble of carriages, an immense morning chorus that mingled with the footsteps of the pedestrians and the cracks of the coachmen's whips. This noisy traffic everywhere put me in a brighter mood immediately, and I started feeling more and more contented. Nothing was further from my mind than just taking a morning walk in the fresh air. What did my lungs care about fresh air? I was strong as a giant and could stop a coach with my bare shoulders. A strange, delicate mood, a feeling of cheerful nonchalance, had taken possession of me. I began to observe the people I met or passed, read the posters on the walls, caught a glance cast my way from a passing streetcar, and laid myself open to every trivial occurrence – all the little fortuitous things that crossed my path and disappeared.

If only one had a bite to eat on such a clear day! Overwhelmed by the impression of the happy morning, I experienced an irrepressible sense of well-being and started humming for joy for no particular reason. A woman with a basket on her arm stood outside a butcher shop pondering sausages for dinner; she glanced at me as I walked past. She had only a single tooth in the front of her mouth. Nervous and susceptible as I had become during the last few days, the woman's face made a repellent impression on me right off; that long yellow tooth looked like a little finger sticking up from her jaw, and her eyes were still full of sausage as she turned toward me. I lost my appetite instantly and felt nauseated. When I reached the Arcades I went over to the fountain and drank some water. I looked up – the clock in the tower of Our Saviour's showed ten.

Continuing through the streets, I roamed about without a care in the world, stopped at a corner without having to, turned and went down a side street without an errand there. I went with the flow, borne from place to place this happy morning, rocking serenely to and fro among other happy people. The sky was clear and bright, and my mind was without a shadow.

For ten minutes now I had constantly had a limping old man ahead of me. In one hand he carried a bundle, and he walked with his whole body, using all his strength to press ahead. I could hear how he panted from the effort, and it occurred to me that I could carry his bundle; still, I didn't try to catch up with him. On Grænsen Street I ran into Hans Pauli, who greeted me and hurried past. Why was he in such a hurry? I certainly didn't mean to ask him for a handout, and I would also presently return a blanket I had borrowed from him a few weeks ago. Once I had pulled through, I certainly didn't want to owe anybody a blanket; I might start an article this very day about the crimes of the future or the freedom of the will, anything whatever, something worth reading, something I would get at least ten kroner for. . . . And at the thought of this article I instantly felt an onrush of desire to begin right away, tapping my chock-full brain. I would find myself a suitable place in Palace Park and not rest till it was finished.

But the old cripple was still making the same wriggling movements up the street ahead of me. In the end I was getting increasingly irritated by having this decrepit creature in front of me all the time. His journey would never end, it seemed; maybe he was going to the exact same place as I, and I would have him before my eyes all the way. Agitated as I was, he appeared to me to slow down a little at each side street and somehow waited to see what direction I would take, whereupon he swung his bundle high in the air once more and walked on with all his might to gain distance on me. I go on watching this bustling fellow and feel my resentment toward him swelling within me. I felt he was slowly ruining my cheery mood and dragging this pure, lovely morning down with him, into ugliness, as well. He looked like a large hobbling insect bent on grabbing a place in the world through brute force and keeping the sidewalk all for itself. When we had reached the top of the hill I refused to put up with it any longer and, turning toward a shop window, stopped to give him an opportunity to slip away. But when I started off again after a few minutes, the man popped up in front of me once more: he too had stood stock-still. Without thinking, I took three or four furious strides forward, caught up with him and tapped him on the shoulder.

He stopped short. We both stared at each other.

'A bit of change for milk!' he finally said, cocking his head.

Well, now I was really in for it! I fumbled in my pockets and said, 'For milk, right. Hmm. Money is scarce these days, and I don't know how badly you may need it.'

'I haven't eaten since yesterday, in Drammen,' the man said. 'I don't have a penny and I'm still out of work.'

'Are you an artisan?'

'Yes, I am a welter.'

'A what?'

'A welter. For that matter, I can make shoes, too.'

'That alters the case,' I said. 'Just wait a few minutes and I'll go and get some money for you, a few øre anyway.'

I hastened down Pilestrædet Lane, where I knew of a pawnbroker on the second floor, someone I had never been to before. When I got inside the gate I quickly took off my waistcoat, rolled it up and stuck it under my arm; then I walked up the stairs and knocked on the door to the shop. I made a bow and threw the waistcoat on the counter.

'One krone and a half,' the man said.

'All right,' I said. 'If it weren't for the fact that it's getting a bit tight for me, I wouldn't have parted with it.'

I got the money and the slip and retraced my steps. All things considered, this business with the waistcoat was an excellent idea; there would even be money to spare for an ample breakfast, and by evening my monograph about the crimes of the future would be ready. Life began to look sunnier right away, and I hastened back to the man to get rid of him.

'Here you are,' I said to him. 'I'm glad you came to me first.'

He took the money and began to look me up and

down. What did he stand there staring at? I had the impression that he examined especially the knees of my trousers, and I found this piece of impudence tiresome. Did that louse imagine I was really as poor as I looked? Hadn't I just about started writing a ten-krone article? On the whole, I had no apprehensions about the future, I had many irons in the fire. So, what business was it of this total stranger if I handed out a gratuity on such a bright morning? The man's stare annoyed me, and I decided to give him a piece of my mind before leaving him. Shrugging my shoulders, I said, 'My dear man, you have fallen into a nasty habit of staring at a man's knees when he gives you a krone's worth of money.'

He leaned his head back against the wall, all the way, and opened his mouth wide. Something was stirring behind that tramp's forehead of his; thinking, no doubt, that I meant to trick him in some way, he handed the money back to me.

I stamped my feet, swearing he should keep it. Did he imagine I had gone to all that trouble for nothing? When all was said and done, maybe I owed him this krone – I had a knack for remembering old debts, he was in the presence of a person of integrity, honest to his very fingertips. In short, the money was his. . . . No need for thanks, it had been a pleasure. Goodbye.

I left. I was rid at last of this paralytic nuisance and could feel at ease. I went down Pilestrædet Lane again and stopped outside a grocer's. The window was packed with food, and I decided to go in and get myself something for the road.

'A piece of cheese and a white loaf!' I said, smacking my half krone down on the counter.

'Cheese and bread for all of it?' the woman asked ironically, without looking at me.

'For all of fifty øre, yes,' I replied, unruffled.

I got my things, said goodbye to the fat old woman with the utmost politeness, and started up Palace Hill to the park without delay. I found a bench for myself and began gnawing greedily at my snack. It did me a lot of good; it had been a long time since I'd had such an ample meal, and I gradually felt that same sense of satiated repose you experience after a good cry. My courage rose markedly; I was no longer satisfied with writing an article about something so elementary and straightforward as the crimes of the future, which anybody could guess, or simply learn by reading history. I felt capable of a greater effort and, being in the mood to surmount difficulties, decided upon a three-part monograph about philosophical cognition. Needless to say, I would have an opportunity to deal a deathblow to Kant's sophisms. . . . When I wanted to get out my writing materials to begin work, I discovered I didn't have a pencil on me any more – I had left it in the pawnshop, my pencil was in the vest pocket.

God, how everything I touched seemed bent on going wrong! I reeled off a few curses, got up from the bench and strolled along the paths, back and forth. It was very quiet everywhere; way over at the Queen's Pavilion a couple of nursemaids were wheeling their baby carriages about, otherwise not a single person could be seen anywhere. I felt extremely angry and paced like a madman up and down in front of my bench. Strange how badly things were going for me wherever I turned! A three-part article would come to nothing simply because I didn't have a ten-øre pencil in my pocket! What if I went down to Pilestrædet Lane again and got my pencil back! There would still be time to complete a sizable portion before the park began to be overrun by pedestrians. So much depended on this monograph about philosophical cognition, maybe several people's happiness, you never knew. I told myself that it might turn out to be a great help to many young people. On second thoughts, I would not attack Kant; it could be avoided, after all – I just had to make an imperceptible detour when I came to the problem of time and space; but I wouldn't answer for Renan, that old parson. . . . At all events, what had to be done was to write an article filling so and so many columns; the unpaid rent and my landlady's long looks when I met her on the stairs in the morning tormented me all day and popped up even in my happy moments, when there wasn't another dark thought in my head. This had to be stopped. I walked rapidly out of the park to pick up my pencil at the pawnbroker's.

When I got as far as Palace Hill I overtook and passed two ladies. As I walked by I brushed the sleeve of one of them; I looked up – she had a full, somewhat pale face. Suddenly she blushes and becomes wonderfully beautiful, I don't know why, maybe from a word she'd heard spoken by a passer-by, maybe only because of some silent thought of her own. Or could it be because I had touched her arm? Her high bosom heaves visibly several times, and she presses her hand firmly around the handle of her parasol. What was the matter with her?

I stopped and let her get ahead of me again – I couldn't continue just then, it all seemed so strange. I was in an irritable mood, annoyed with myself because of the mishap with the pencil and highly stimulated by all the food I had put away on an empty stomach. All at once my thoughts, by a fanciful whim, take an odd direction – I'm seized by a strange desire to frighten this lady, to follow her and hurt her in some way. I overtake her once more and walk past her, then abruptly turn around and meet her face to face to observe her. I stand there looking her straight in the eye, and immediately a name comes to me, one I had never heard before, a name with a nervous, gliding sound: Ylajali. Once she is close enough to me, I straighten up and say urgently, 'Miss, you're losing your book.'

I could hear the sound of my heartbeat as I said it.

'My book?' she asks her companion. And she walks on.

My malice increased and I followed the lady. I was at that moment fully conscious of playing a mad prank, without being able to do anything about it; my confused state was running away with me, giving me the most insane ideas, which I obeyed one after the other. No matter how much I kept telling myself that I was behaving like an idiot, it was no use; I made the stupidest faces behind the lady's back and coughed furiously several times as I walked past her. Strolling on thus at a slow pace, always with a few steps' lead, I could feel her eyes on my back and instinctively ducked with shame at having pestered her. Gradually I began to have an odd sensation of being far away, in some other place; I vaguely felt that it wasn't I who was walking there on the flagstones with bowed head.

A few minutes later the lady has reached Pascha's Bookshop. I'm already standing at the first window, and as she walks by I step out and say again, 'Miss, you're losing your book.'

'What book?' she asks, scared. 'Can you understand what book he's talking about?'

She stops. I gloat cruelly over her confusion, the bewilderment in her eyes gives me a thrill. Her thoughts cannot fathom my little desperate remark; she has no book at all with her, not a single page of a book, and yet she searches her pockets, looks repeatedly at her hands, turns her head to examine the street behind her, and racks her sensitive little brain to the utmost to find out what sort of book I am talking about. Her colour comes and goes, her face changes from one expression to another, and her breath is audible; even the buttons on her dress seem to stare at me, like a row of terrified eyes.

'Don't mind him,' her companion says, pulling her by the arm; 'he's drunk. Can't you see the man is drunk!'

However estranged I was from myself at this moment, so completely at the mercy of invisible influences, nothing that was taking place around me escaped my perception. A big brown dog ran across the street, toward the Students' Promenade and down to the amusement park; it had a narrow collar of German silver. Farther up the street a window was opened on the second floor and a maid with her sleeves turned up leaned out and began to clean the panes on the outside. Nothing escaped my attention, I was lucid and self-possessed, and everything rushed in upon me with a brilliant distinctness, as if an intense light had suddenly sprung up around me. The ladies before me had each a blue-bird's wing in their hats and a plaid silk band around their necks. It occurred to me that they were sisters.

Turning aside, they stopped at Cisler's Music Shop and talked. I stopped also. Then they both started back, going the same way they had come, passed me once again, turned the corner at University Street and went straight up to St Olaf Place. All the while I followed as hard upon their heels as I dared. They turned around once, giving me a half-scared, half-curious glance; I didn't perceive any resentment in their looks nor any knitted brows. This patience with my harassment made me feel very ashamed, and I lowered my eyes. I didn't want to pester them any more – I would follow them with my eyes out of sheer gratitude, not lose sight of them until they entered somewhere and disappeared.

In front of number 2, a big four-storey building, they turned once more and then went in. I leaned against a lamppost near the fountain and listened for their footsteps on the stairs; they died away on the second floor. I step out from under the lamp and look up at the building. Then something odd happens – high up some curtains stir, a moment later a window is opened, a head pops out, and two strange-looking eyes are fixed on me. 'Ylajali,' I said under my breath, feeling myself turning red. Why didn't she call for help? Why didn't she push one of those flowerpots over on my head or send someone down to chase me away? We stand looking each other straight in the face without moving; a minute goes by; thoughts dart back and forth between the window and the street, but not a word is spoken. She turns around – I feel a jolt, a light shock, go through me; I see a shoulder turning, a back disappearing into the room. This unhurried stepping away from the window, the inflection of that movement of her shoulder, was like a nod to me; my blood perceived this subtle greeting and I felt wonderfully happy all at once. Then I turned around and walked down the street.

Not daring to look back, I didn't know if she had come to the window again; as I pondered this question I grew more and more uneasy and nervous. In all likelihood she was at this moment closely following every movement of mine, and it was absolutely unbearable to know that you were being scrutinised like that from behind. I pulled myself together as best I could and walked on; my legs began twitching and my walk became unsteady just because I purposely tried to make it graceful. In order to seem calm and indifferent I waved my arms absurdly, spat at the ground and stuck my nose in the air, but it was no use. I constantly felt those pursuing eyes on my neck and a chill went through my body. At last I took refuge in a side street, from which I set off for Pilestrædet Lane to get hold of my pencil.

I didn't have any trouble retrieving it. The man brought me the waistcoat himself and invited me to go through all the pockets while I was at it. I did find a couple of pawn tickets, which I pocketed, and thanked the friendly man for his courtesy. I liked him more and more, and it became very important to me at that moment to make a good impression on him. I started walking toward the door but turned back to the counter again as if I had forgotten something; I felt I owed him an explanation, a bit of information, and began humming to catch his attention. Then I took the pencil into my hand and held it up.

It would never occur to me, I said, to come such a long way for just any pencil; but with this one it was a different matter, there was a special reason. However insignificant it might look, this stump of a pencil had simply made me what I was in this world, had put me in my right place in life, so to speak. . . .

I didn't say any more. The man came right up to the counter.

'Is that so?' he said, looking curiously at me.

With this pencil, I continued coolly, I had written my monograph about philosophical cognition in three volumes. Hadn't he heard of it?

And the man thought that, sure enough, he had heard the name, the title.

Well, I said, that one was by me, yes indeed! So he shouldn't be at all surprised that I wanted to get this tiny stub of a pencil back; it was far too precious to me, it seemed almost like a little person. Anyway, I was sincerely grateful to him for his kindness and would remember him for it – oh yes, I would really remember him for it; a word was a word, that was the kind of person I was, and he deserved it. Goodbye.

I probably walked to the door with the bearing of someone having the power to make a high appointment. The respectable pawnbroker bowed twice to me as I withdrew, and I turned once more to say goodbye.

On the stairs I met a woman carrying a travelling bag in her hand. She timidly pressed closer to the wall to make room for me since I was giving myself such airs, and I instinctively put my hand in my pocket for something to give her. When I didn't find anything I felt embarrassed and ducked my head as I passed her. Shortly afterward I heard her, too, knocking at the door of the shop – the door had a steel-wire grille on it, and I immediately recognised the jingling sound it made when touched by human knuckles.

The sun was in the south, it was about twelve. The city was beginning to get on its feet; with strolling time approaching, bowing and laughing people were surging up and down Karl Johan Street. I pressed my elbows against my sides to make myself small and slipped unnoticed past some acquaintances who had stationed themselves at a corner by the University to watch the passers-by. I wandered up Palace Hill and became lost in thought.

These people that I met – how lightly and merrily they bobbed their bright faces, dancing their way through life as though it were a ballroom! There was no sign of grief in a single eye that I saw, no burden on any shoulder, not even a cloudy thought maybe, or a little secret suffering, in any of those happy hearts. While I, who walked there right beside these people, young and freshly blown, had already forgotten the very look of happiness! Coddling myself with this thought, I found that a terrible injustice had been done to me. Why had these last few months been so exceedingly rough on me? I couldn't recognise my cheerful disposition anymore, and I had the weirdest troubles wherever I turned. I couldn't sit down on a bench by myself or set foot anywhere without being attacked by small, trivial incidents, miserable trifles that forced their way among my ideas and scattered my powers to the four winds. A dog streaking past, a yellow rose in a gentleman's buttonhole, could start my thoughts vibrating and occupy me for a long time. What was the matter with me? Had the Lord's finger pointed at me? But why exactly me? Why not just as well at some person in South America, for that matter? When I pondered this, it became more and more incomprehensible to me why precisely I should have been chosen as a guinea pig for a caprice of divine grace. To skip a whole world in order to get to me – that was a rather odd way of doing things; there was, after all, both Pascha the second-hand book dealer and Hennechen, the steamship agent.

I wandered about debating this matter, unable to get it out of my mind; I discovered the weightiest objections to the Lord's arbitrariness in letting me suffer for everybody else's sake. Even after I had found a bench and sat down, this question continued to occupy me, hindering me from thinking about anything else. From that day in May when my adversities had begun I could clearly perceive a gradually increasing weakness, I seemed to have become too feeble to steer or guide myself where I wanted to go; a swarm of tiny vermin had forced its way inside me and hollowed me out. What if God simply intended to annihilate me? I stood up and paced back and forth in front of my bench.

My whole being was at this moment filled with the utmost anguish; even my arms ached, and I could barely endure carrying them in the usual way. I also felt a marked discomfort from my recent big meal. Glutted and irritated, I walked to and fro without looking up;

the people who came and went around me glided by like flickering shadows. Finally my bench was taken by a couple of gentlemen who lighted their cigars and chatted loudly; I became angry and meant to speak to them, but turned around and went all the way to the other end of the park, where I found another bench for myself. I sat down.

The thought of God began to occupy me again. It seemed to me quite inexcusable for him to meddle every time I applied for a job and thus upset everything, since all I was asking for was my daily bread. I had noticed distinctly that every time I went hungry for quite a long time it was as though my brain trickled quietly out of my head, leaving me empty. My head grew light and absent, I could no longer feel its weight on my shoulders, and I had the impression that my eyes showed a too-wide stare when I looked at somebody.

As I sat there on the bench pondering all this, I felt increasingly bitter toward God for his continual oppressions. If he meant to draw me closer to himself and make me better by torturing me and casting adversity my way, he was simply mistaken, that I could vouch for. And nearly crying with defiance, I looked up toward heaven and told him so once and for all, inwardly.

Fragments of my childhood teachings came back to me, the cadences of the Bible rang in my ears, and I spoke softly to myself, cocking my head sarcastically. Wherefore did I take thought what I should eat, what I should drink, and wherewithal I should clothe this wretched bag of worms called my earthly body? Had not my heavenly Father provided for me as he had for the sparrows of the air, and had he not shown me the grace of pointing at his humble servant? God had stuck his finger down into the network of my nerves and gently, quite casually, brought a little confusion among the threads. And God had withdrawn his finger and behold! – there were fibres and delicate filaments on his finger from the threads of my nerves. And there was a gaping hole after his finger, which was God's finger, and wounds in my brain from the track of his finger. But where God had touched me with the finger of his hand he let me be and touched me no more, and allowed no evil to befall me. He let me go in peace, and he let me go with that gaping hole. And no evil shall befall me from God, who is the Lord through all eternity. . . .

Gusts of music are borne on the wind toward me from the Students' Promenade. So it must be after two. I got out my paper and things to try and write something, and as I did so my book of shaving coupons fell out of my pocket. I opened it and counted the pages – there were six coupons left. Thank God! I burst out; I could still get myself a shave for several weeks and look presentable! My spirits rose immediately because of this little possession that I still had left; I smoothed the coupons out carefully and put the book away in my pocket.

But write – no, I couldn't do it. After a few lines nothing more occurred to me; my thoughts were elsewhere and I couldn't pull myself together to make any definite effort. I was acted on and distracted by everything around me, all that I saw gave me new impressions. Flies and gnats stuck to the paper and disturbed me; I blew on them to make them go away, then blew harder and harder, but it was no use. The little pests lean back and make themselves heavy, putting up such a struggle that their thin legs bend. They just cannot be made to budge. Having found something to latch onto, they brace their heels against a comma or an unevenness in the paper and stand stock-still until they find it convenient to take off.

These little monsters continued to occupy me for quite a while, and I crossed my legs and took my time observing them. All at once a couple of loud, piercing clarinet notes reached me from the Students' Promenade, giving my thoughts a fresh impetus. Discouraged at not being able to prepare my article, I stuck the papers in my pocket again and leaned back on the bench. At this moment my head is so clear that I can think the most subtle thoughts without tiring. As I lie there in this position, letting my eyes wander down my breast and legs, I notice the twitching motion made by my foot at each beat of my pulse. I sit up halfway and look down at my feet, and at this moment I experience a fantastic, alien state I'd never felt before; a delicate, mysterious thrill spreads through my nerves, as though they were flooded by surges of light. When I looked at my shoes, it was as though I had met a good friend or got back a torn-off part of me: a feeling of recognition trembles through all my senses, tears spring to my eyes, and I perceive my shoes as a softly murmuring tune coming toward me. Weakness! I said harshly to myself, and I clenched my fists and said: Weakness. I mocked myself for these ridiculous feelings, made fun of myself quite consciously; I spoke very sternly and reasonably, and I fiercely squeezed my eyes shut to get rid of my tears. Then I begin, as though I'd never seen my shoes before, to study their appearance, their mimicry when I move my feet, their shape and the worn uppers, and I discover that their wrinkles and their white seams give them an expression, lend them a physiognomy. Something of my own nature had entered into these shoes – they affected me like a breath upon my being, a living, breathing part of me. . . .

I sat there indulging my fancy with these perceptions for quite a while, perhaps a whole hour. A little old man came up and occupied the other end of my bench; as he sat down he drew a heavy sigh after his walk and said, 'Ay-ay-ay-ay-ay me!'

As soon as I heard his voice, it was as though a wind swept through my head. I let shoes remain shoes, and it now seemed to me that the confused state of mind I had just experienced belonged to a time long past, perhaps a year or two ago, and was slowly getting erased from my memory. I set about observing the old fellow.

What concern was he of mine, this little man? None, none at all! Except that he was holding a newspaper in his hand, an old issue with the ad page up front in which something seemed to be wrapped up. I became curious and couldn't take my eyes off that paper; I had the insane idea that it might be an unusual newspaper, in a class by itself; my curiosity increased and I began to slide back and forth on the bench. It might contain documents, dangerous records stolen from some archive! The thought of some secret treaty, a plot, hovered before me.

The man sat still, thinking. Why didn't he carry his paper the way every other person did, with its name on the outside? What sort of tricks was he up to? It didn't look like he would ever let go of his parcel, not for anything in the world, he might even be afraid to entrust it to his own pocket. I could bet my life there was more to this matter of the parcel than met the eye.

I gazed straight ahead of me. The very fact that it was so impossible to penetrate this mysterious affair made me beside myself with curiosity. I searched my pockets for something I could give the man in order to start a conversation with him; I got hold of my shaving book but put it away again. Suddenly I took it into my head to be utterly shameless, patted my empty breast pocket and said, 'May I offer you a cigarette?'

No thanks, the man didn't smoke, he'd had to give up to spare his eyes – he was nearly blind. 'But many thanks anyway!'

Had his eyes been ailing for a long time? Then he couldn't even read maybe? Not even the papers?

Not even the papers, he was sorry to say.

The man looked at me. Those sick eyes were each covered with a film which gave them a glazed look; they appeared whitish and made a repellent impression.

'You're a stranger here?' he said.

'Yes.' Couldn't he even read the name of the paper he was holding in his hand?

'Hardly.' Anyway, he had heard right away that I was a stranger, something in my accent had told him. It took so little, his hearing was very good; at night when everybody was asleep he could hear the people in the next room breathing. . . . 'What I wanted to ask was, where do you live?'

A lie appeared fully fledged in my head on the spur

of the moment. I lied automatically, without meaning to and with no ulterior motive, and replied, 'At 2 St Olaf Place.'

'Really?' The man knew every stone in St Olaf Place. There was a fountain, some street lamps, a couple of trees, he remembered it all. . . . 'What number do you live at?'

Wanting to make an end of it, I got up, driven to extremities by my idea about the newspaper. The secret had to be cleared up, no matter the cost.

'If you can't read that paper, then why—?'

'At number 2, did you say?' the man went on, without paying any attention to my restlessness. 'At one time I used to know every person in number 2. What's the name of your landlord?'

I hit upon a name in a hurry to get rid of him, a name made up on the spot, and spat it out to stop my tormentor.

'Happolati,' I said.

'Happolati, yes,' the man nodded, without losing a syllable of this difficult name.

I looked at him with amazement; he appeared very serious, with a thoughtful air. No sooner had I uttered this stupid name that had popped into my head than the man was comfortable with it and pretended to have heard it before. Meanwhile he put his parcel away on the bench, and I felt my nerves tingling with curiosity. I noticed that there were a couple of grease spots on the paper.

'Isn't he a sailor, your landlord?' the man asked, without a trace of irony in his voice. 'I seem to remember that he was a sailor.'

'A sailor? Pardon me, it must be his brother that you know; this, you see, is J.A. Happolati, the agent.'

I thought that would finish him off, but the man acquiesced in everything.

'He's supposed to be an able man, I've heard,' he said, feeling his way.

'Oh, a shrewd man,' I replied, 'a real business capacity, agent for all sorts of things, lingonberries to China, feathers and down from Russia, hides, wood pulp, writing ink—'

'Hee-hee, I'll be damned!' the old man broke in, extremely animated.

This was beginning to get interesting. The situation was running away with me, and one lie after another sprang up in my head. I sat down again, forgot about the paper and the remarkable documents, became excited and interrupted him when he spoke. The little dwarf's gullibility made me reckless, I felt like stuffing him full of lies come what may, driving him from the field in grand style.

Had he heard about the electric hymn book that Happolati had invented?

'What, an elec—?'

With electric letters that shone in the dark? A quite magnificent enterprise, millions of kroner involved, foundries and printing shops in operation, hosts of salaried mechanics employed, as many as seven hundred men, I'd heard.

'Just as I have always said,' the man remarked, softly. That was all he said; he believed every word I had told him and still wasn't bowled over. This disappointed me a little, I had expected to see him utterly bewildered by my inventions.

I came up with a couple of other desperate lies, taking a mad gamble by hinting that Happolati had been a cabinet minister in Persia for nine years. 'You may not have any idea what it means to be a cabinet minister in Persia,' I said. It was more than being king here, about the same as a sultan, if he knew what that was. But Happolati had managed it all and was never at a loss. And I told him about Ylajali, his daughter, a fairy princess who owned three hundred women slaves and slept on a bed of yellow roses; she was the loveliest creature I had ever seen, I hadn't seen anything in all my life that matched her loveliness, God strike me dead if I had!

'She was that pretty, was she?' the old man remarked with an absent air, looking down at the ground.

Pretty? She was gorgeous, she was ravishingly sweet! Eyes like raw silk, arms of amber! A single glance from her was as seductive as a kiss, and when she called me her voice went straight to my heart, like a jet of wine. And why shouldn't she be that beautiful? Did he think she was a bill collector or something or other in the fire brigade? She was simply divine, he could take it from me, a fairy tale.

'I see,' the man said, somewhat confused.

His composure bored me; I had become excited by the sound of my own voice and spoke in deadly earnest. The stolen archival papers, the treaty with some foreign power or other, these no longer occupied my thoughts; the little flat parcel lay there on the bench between us, but I no longer had the least desire to examine it and see what was in it. I was completely taken up with my own tales, wonderful visions hovered before my eyes, the blood rushed to my head and I lied like a trooper.

At this moment the man seemed to want to leave. Raising his body slightly, he asked, so as not to break off the conversation too abruptly, 'This Mr Happolati is supposed to own vast properties, isn't he?'

How did this disgusting, blind old fool dare play around with the foreign name I had invented, as if it was just an ordinary name, one you could see on any huckster's sign in town! He never stumbled over a single letter and never forgot a syllable; this name had taken firm hold of his brain and struck root instantly. I felt chagrined, and indignation began to arise in my heart against this person whom nothing could baffle and nothing make suspicious.

And so I replied, grumpily, 'That I'm not aware of; in fact, I'm not aware of that at all. And by the way, let me tell you once and for all that his name is Johan Arendt Happolati, judging by his initials.'

'Johan Arendt Happolati,' the man repeated, surprised by my vehemence. Then he was silent.

'You should've seen his wife,' I said furiously. 'A fatter woman—. Or perhaps you don't believe she was really fat?'

Oh yes, of course he did – a man like that—.

The old fellow replied meekly and quietly to every one of my sallies, searching for words as if he were afraid to say something wrong and make me angry.

'Hell's teeth, man, perhaps you think I'm sitting here stuffing you chock-full of lies?' I cried, beside myself.

'Perhaps you don't even believe that a man with the name Happolati exists! What obstinacy and wickedness in an old man – I've never seen the likes of it. What the hell is the matter with you? Perhaps, on top of everything, you've been thinking to yourself that I must be a terribly poor fellow, sitting here in my Sunday best without a well-stocked cigarette case in my pocket? Let me tell you, sir, that I'm not at all accustomed to such treatment as yours, and I won't stand for it, God strike me dead if I do, either from you or from anyone else. Now you know!'

The man had gotten to his feet. His mouth agape, he stood there speechless, listening to my outburst until it was over. Then he quickly picked up his parcel from the bench and left, all but running down the path with short, old man's steps.

I sat watching his back, which gradually receded and seemed to stoop more and more. I don't know where the impression came from, but it appeared to me that I had never seen a more dishonest, vicious back than this one, and I wasn't at all sorry that I had given the creature a piece of my mind before he left. . . .

The day was on the wane, the sun was sinking, a soft rustle arose in the trees round about, and the nursemaids sitting in groups over by the seesaw were getting ready to push their baby carriages home. I was calm and felt at ease. The excitement I had just been through gradually subsided; I slumped over, grew limp, and began to feel sleepy. Nor was the large amount of bread I had eaten doing me any great harm any more. In the best of moods, I leaned back on the bench, closed my eyes and felt more and more drowsy; I dozed off, and I was on the point of falling fast asleep when a park attendant placed his hand on my shoulder and said, 'You can't sit and sleep in here.'

'No,' I said, getting up instantly. At one blow my whole wretched situation rose vividly before my eyes once more. I had to do something, come up with some idea or other. To apply for a job hadn't been any use; the reference letters I presented were old by now and written by people who were too little known to carry much weight; besides, these constant refusals all summer long had made me timid. Well, at any rate my rent was due and I had to find some way to pay it. The rest would have to wait a while.

Quite instinctively, I had again got paper and pencil into my hands, and I sat and wrote mechanically the date 1848 in every corner of the page. If only a single scintillating thought would come, grip me utterly, and put words in my mouth! It had happened before after all, it had really happened that such moments came over me, so that I could write a long piece without effort and get it wonderfully right.

I sit there on the bench and write 1848 dozens of times; I write this number criss-cross in all possible shapes and wait for a usable idea to occur to me. A swarm of loose thoughts is fluttering about in my head. The mood of the dying day makes me despondent and sentimental. Autumn has arrived and has already begun to put every-thing into a deep sleep; flies and other insects have suffered their first setback, and up in the trees and down on the ground you can hear the sounds of struggling life, pottering, ceaselessly rustling, labouring not to perish. All crawling things are stirring once more; they stick their yellow heads out of the moss, lift their legs and grope their way with their long feelers, before they suddenly give out, rolling over and turning up their bellies. Every growing thing has received its distinctive mark, a gentle breath of the first frost; the grass stems, stiff and pale, strain upwards towards the sun, and the fallen leaves rustle along the ground with a sound like that of wandering silkworms. It's autumn, the very carnival of transience; the roses have an inflamed flush, their blood-red colour tinged with a wonderfully hectic hue.

I felt I was myself a crawling insect doomed to perish, seized by destruction in the midst of a whole world ready to go to sleep. Possessed by strange terrors, I stood up and took several whopping strides down the path. 'No!' I shouted, clenching my fists, 'this has to end!' And I sat down again, picked up my pencil once more and was ready to attack my article in earnest. It would never do to give up when the unpaid rent was staring me in the face.

My thoughts gradually began to compose themselves. Taking great care, I wrote slowly a couple of well-considered pages, an introduction to something; it could serve as the beginning to almost anything, whether a travelogue or a political article, depending on what I felt like doing. It was an excellent beginning to something or other.

Then I began to look for a definite question that I could deal with, some person or thing I could tackle, but I didn't come up with anything. During this fruitless effort my thoughts began to get confused again – I felt my brain literally snap, my head was emptying and emptying, and in the end it sat light and void on my shoulders. I perceived this gaping emptiness in my head with my whole body, I felt hollowed out from top to toe.

'Lord, my God and Father!' I cried in agony, and I repeated this cry several times in succession without adding a word.

The wind fluttered the leaves, a storm was brewing. I sat a while longer, staring forlornly at my papers, then I folded them and put them slowly in my pocket. It was getting chilly and I didn't have a waistcoat any more; I buttoned my coat up to the neck and stuck my hands in my pockets. Then I got up and left.

If only I had succeeded this time, this one time! Twice now my landlady had asked me for payment with her eyes, and I'd had to duck my head and sneak past her with an embarrassed greeting. I couldn't do that again; the next time I met those eyes I would give notice and explain myself in all honesty. It couldn't continue like this in the long run anyhow.

When I got to the exit of the park I again saw the old dwarf I had put to flight in my rage. The mysterious newspaper parcel lay open on the bench beside him, with lots of different kinds of food that he was munching on. I wanted to go and apologise to him right away, ask his forgiveness for my behaviour, but his food turned me off. Those aged fingers, looking like ten wrinkled claws, were clutching the greasy sandwiches in their disgusting grip; I felt nauseated and walked by without addressing him. He didn't recognise me – his eyes, dry as horn, just stared at me, and his face didn't move a muscle.

I walked on.

As was my wont, I stopped at every posted newspaper that I passed to study the notices of job openings, and I was lucky enough to find one I could fill: a shopkeeper on Grønlandsleret Street wanted someone for a couple of hours' bookkeeping every evening; wages by agreement. I took down the person's address and prayed silently to God for this job – I would ask less than anyone else for the work, fifty øre was plenty, or perhaps forty øre, come what may.

When I got home there was a note on my table from the landlady in which she asked me to pay my rent in advance or move out as soon as I could. I mustn't mind her telling me, it was nothing but a necessary request. Cordially, Mrs Gundersen.

I wrote an application to Christie's, the shopkeeper, at 31 Grønlandsleret Street, put it in an envelope and took it down to the mailbox at the corner. Then I went back up to my room and sat down to think in my rocking chair, while the darkness grew more and more impenetrable. It was beginning to be difficult to stay up now.

The next morning I awoke very early. It was still quite dark when I opened my eyes, and only much later did I hear the clock in the downstairs apartment strike five. I wanted to go to sleep again but wasn't able to, I felt more and more awake and lay there thinking about a million things.

Suddenly one or two good sentences occur to me, suitable for a sketch or story, nice linguistic flukes the likes of which I had never experienced before. I lie there repeating these words to myself and find that they are excellent. Presently they're joined by others, I'm at once wide awake, sit up and grab paper and pencil from the table behind my bed. It was as though a vein had burst inside me – one word follows another, they connect with one another and turn into situations; scenes pile on top of other scenes, actions and dialogue well up in my brain, and a wonderful sense of pleasure takes hold of me. I write as if possessed, filling one page after another without a moment's pause. My thoughts strike me so suddenly and continue to pour out so abundantly that I lose a lot of minor details I'm not able to write down fast enough, though I am working at full blast. They continue to crowd in on me, I am full of my subject, and every word I write is put in my mouth.

It goes on and on, it takes such a wonderfully long time before this singular moment ceases to be; I have 15 to 20 written pages lying on my knees in front of me when I finally stop and put my pencil away. Now, if these pages were really worth something, then I was saved! I jump out of bed and get dressed. It is growing lighter and lighter and I can dimly make out the notice from the Director of Lighthouses over by the door, and at the window there is already enough daylight so I could see to write, at a pinch. I start making a clean copy of my pages right away.

A strange dense vapour of light and colour rises up from these fantasies; I'm agog with surprise seeing one good thing after another, telling myself that it is the best thing I have ever read. Elated with a sense of fulfillment and puffed up with joy, I feel on top of the world. I weigh the piece in my hand and appraise it on the spot at five kroner, by a rough estimate. It wouldn't occur to anybody to haggle about five kroner; on the contrary, judging by the quality of the contents one would have to call it a bargain at ten. I had no intention of undertaking such a special piece of work for nothing; as far as I knew, you didn't find stories like that by the wayside. I decided in favour of ten kroner.

It was growing lighter and lighter in the room; glancing toward the door, I could read without great difficulty the fine, skeleton-like letters concerning Madam Andersen's shrouds, main entrance to the right. Anyway, the clock had struck seven a good while ago.

I got up and stood in the middle of the floor. Everything considered, Mrs Gundersen's notice was quite opportune. This wasn't really a room for me; the green curtains before the windows were rather tawdry, and there was anything but an abundance of nails on the walls for hanging one's wardrobe. That poor rocking chair over in the corner was actually only a poor excuse for a rocking chair, you could easily laugh yourself sick at it. It was much too low for a grown man, and so tight that you had to use a bootjack, so to speak, to get back out of it. In short, the room wasn't furnished with an eye to intellectual pursuits, and I did not intend to keep it any longer. I wouldn't keep it under any circumstances! I had been silent all too long, putting up with living in this dump.

Puffed up with hope and self-satisfaction and constantly absorbed by my interesting sketch, which I pulled out of my pocket to read every now and then, I decided to buckle down at once and get going with my move.

I took out my bundle, a red handkerchief that contained a couple of clean collars and some crumpled newspapers I had carried my bread home in, rolled up my blanket and pocketed my stack of white writing paper. Then, to be on the safe side, I inspected every corner of the room to make sure I hadn't forgotten anything, and when nothing turned up I went over to the window and looked out. The morning was wet and gloomy; no one had shown up at the burned-down blacksmith's shop, and the clothesline down in the courtyard hung taut from wall to wall, shrunken by the wetness. I knew it all from before, so I stepped away from the window, took the blanket under my arm, bowed to the notice from the Director of Lighthouses, bowed to Madam Andersen's shrouds, and opened the door.

Suddenly I remembered about my landlady; she ought to be notified of my moving, so she would know she had been dealing with a respectable person. I also wanted to thank her, in writing, for the couple of extra days I had used the room. The certainty that I was now taken care of for a long time to come impressed itself upon me so strongly that I even promised to give my landlady five kroner when I dropped by one of these days; I would show her with a vengeance what a cultured person she had sheltered under her roof.

I left the note on the table.

I stopped by the door once more and turned around. This glorious feeling of having come out on top enchanted me, making me grateful to God and everyone, and I kneeled down by the bed and thanked God in a loud voice for his great goodness toward me this morning.

I knew – oh yes, I knew that the exalted moment and the inspiration I had just experienced and written down was a wonderful work of heaven in my soul, an answer to my cry of distress yesterday. 'It's God! It's God!' I cried to myself, and I wept from enthusiasm over my own words; every now and then I had to stop and listen for a moment, in case someone should be on the stairs. Finally I stood up and left. I slipped noiselessly down all those flights of stairs and reached the gate unseen.

The streets were glistening with the rain that had fallen in the early morning, the sky hung raw and heavy over the city, and you couldn't see a glimpse of sun anywhere. How late in the day was it? I wondered. I walked as usual in the direction of the city jail and noticed that the clock showed half-past eight. So I had a couple of hours to spare – it was useless to go to the newspaper office before ten, or perhaps eleven; meanwhile I would simply wander about and at the same time devise some means of getting breakfast. Anyway, I had no fear that I would have to go to bed hungry that day; those times were over, thank God! That was a thing of the past, a bad dream, from now on things were looking up!

Meanwhile the green blanket was an inconvenience to me; nor would it do to walk around with a parcel under one's arm in plain sight of everybody. What would people think of me? So I wondered how to find a place where it could be left for safekeeping for a time. Then it occurred to me that I could go over to Semb's and get it wrapped; that would make it look better right away, and there would be nothing to be ashamed of any more in carrying it. I entered the store and stated my errand to one of the clerks.

He looked first at the blanket and then at me. It seemed to me he mentally shrugged his shoulders in contempt as he accepted the parcel. I felt offended.

'Be careful, damn it!' I cried. 'There are two expensive glass vases inside. The parcel is going to Smyrna.'

That helped. It helped a lot. The man begged my pardon in every movement he made for not guessing right away there were important articles inside the blanket. When he had finished his wrapping, I thanked him for his help like someone who had sent precious objects to Smyrna before, and he even opened the door for me when I left.

I began wandering about among the people at Stortorvet Square, preferring to stay close to the women selling potted plants. The heavy red roses, smouldering with a raw, bloody flush this damp morning, made me greedy, and I was sorely tempted to snatch one; I asked the price just so I could get as close to it as possible. If I had money left over I would buy it, come what may; after all, I could always skimp a little here and there on my daily fare to balance my budget again.

Ten o'clock came around and I went to the newspaper office. 'Scissors' is rummaging through some old newspapers, the editor hasn't come in yet. I hand over my big manuscript on request, giving the man to understand that it is of more than merely ordinary importance, and I urge him to remember to hand it to the editor personally when he showed up. I would drop by for his answer myself later in the day.

'Very good!' Scissors said, going back to his newspapers.

I thought he took it all too casually but didn't say anything, just nodded indifferently to him and left.

Now I had plenty of time on my hands. If only it would clear up! The weather was really miserable, without a breath of air or freshness; the ladies were carrying umbrellas just in case and the gentlemen wearing funny-looking woollen caps. I took another turn on Stortorvet Square to look at the vegetables and the roses. Then I feel a hand on my shoulder and turn around: the 'Maiden' says good morning.

'Good morning?' I reply in a questioning tone, in order to know his business right away. I didn't care much for the 'Maiden'.

He looks curiously at the big brand-new parcel under my arm and asks, 'What have you got there?'

'I've been down at Semb's and got some material for clothes,' I answer in a casual tone. 'I thought I shouldn't go around looking so shabby any longer – one can be too mean with one's body, you know.'

He looks at me, surprised.

'How are things, by the way?' he asks hesitantly.

'Oh, beyond expectations.'

'So you've found something to do, have you?'

'Something to do?' I reply, looking greatly surprised. 'I'm bookkeeper at Christie's, the merchant, don't you know?'

'Oh, indeed!' he says, backing away a little. 'Gosh, I'm so happy for you! I just hope they won't wheedle the money you make out of you. Goodbye.'

In a little while he turns around and comes back. Pointing his cane at my parcel, he says, 'I would like to recommend my tailor for your suit of clothes. You won't find a more fashionable tailor than Isaksen. Just say I sent you.'

Why did he have to stick his nose into my affairs? What was it to him which tailor I used? I got angry. The sight of this empty, dolled-up individual made me indignant, and I reminded him rather brutally of the ten kroner he had borrowed from me. However, even before he managed to answer I regretted having pressed him for the money; I became embarrassed and avoided meeting his eyes. When a woman walked by just then, I stepped quickly back to let her pass and used the opportunity to make off.

What should I do with myself while waiting? I couldn't go to a café with empty pockets, and I didn't know of any acquaintance I might look up at this time of day. I headed instinctively uptown, idled away some time going from Stortorvet Square to Grænsen Street, read the number of *Aftenposten* which had just been tacked up on the bulletin board, made a detour down to Karl Johan Street, then turned around and walked straight up to Our Saviour's Cemetery, where I found myself a quiet spot on the rise near the chapel.

I sat there in silence, dozing in the damp air, musing, half asleep and feeling cold. Time passed. Could I be absolutely certain that my story was truly inspired, a little artistic masterpiece? God knows it might have some faults here and there. Everything considered, it didn't even have to get accepted – no, that was it, not even accepted! What if it was quite mediocre or perhaps downright bad; what guarantee did I have that it wasn't at this very moment lying in the wastepaper basket already? . . . My feeling of contentment had been shaken, I jumped up and stormed out of the cemetery.

Down in Aker Street I glanced into a shop window and saw that it was only a few minutes past twelve. This made me even more desperate, having so confidently hoped it was way past noon; there was no use in looking for the editor until four. The fate of my story filled me with dark forebodings; the more I thought about it, the more absurd it seemed that I could have written something usable so suddenly, half asleep at that, my brain full of fever and dreams. I had deceived myself, of course, and been happy all morning for nothing! Of course! . . . I walked briskly up Ullevaal Road, past St Hanshaugen, came onto some open land, then into the quaint narrow lanes in the Sagene section, crossed some empty lots and cultivated fields, and finally found myself on a country road the end of which I couldn't see.

Here I came to a standstill and decided to turn around. I felt warm from my walk and went back slowly, very depressed. I met two hay wagons, the drivers, both bareheaded and with round carefree faces, lying flat on top of their loads and singing. I thought to myself as I walked along that they would be sure to say something, throw some remark or other my way or play a prank, and when I got close enough one of them called out and asked what I had under my arm.

'A blanket,' I replied.

'What time is it?' he asked.

'I don't know exactly, about three, I think.'

Then they both laughed and drove past. At that instant I felt the flick of a whip against my ear, and my hat was twitched off. The youngsters couldn't let me pass without playing a trick on me. I put my hand angrily to my ear, picked up my hat from the edge of the ditch and continued walking. At St Hanshaugen I met a man who told me it was past four.

Past four! It was already past four o'clock! I strode off towards town and the newspaper office. Perhaps the editor had been there ages ago and left the office already! I walked and ran by turns, stumbling and knocking against the carriages, left all the other pedestrians behind and kept pace with the horses, fighting like crazy to get there in time. I wriggled through the gate, took the stairs in four bounds and knocked.

No answer.

I think, He's gone! He's gone! I try the door, it's open. I knock once more and step in.

The editor is sitting at his desk, his face turned towards the window, pen in hand poised to write. When he hears my breathless greeting he turns half around, looks at me for a moment, shakes his head and says, 'I haven't had time to read your sketch yet.'

I feel so glad that at least he hasn't yet scrapped it that I answer, 'Goodness, no, I quite understand. There's no great hurry. In a couple of days maybe, or . . .?'

'Well, we'll see. Anyway, I have your address.'

I forgot to inform him that I no longer had an address.

The audience is over, I step back, bowing, and leave. My hopes are fired up again, nothing was lost yet – on the contrary, I could still win everything, for that matter. And my brain began to fantasise about a great council in heaven where it had just been decided that I should win, win handsomely ten kroner for a story. . . .

If only I had some place to stay for the night! I ponder where I could best slip in, and I become so absorbed by this question that I stand stock-still in the middle of the street. I forget where I am and stand like a solitary buoy in the middle of the ocean, surrounded on all sides by surging, roaring waves. A newsboy holds out a copy of *Vikingen* to me: 'It's such fun!' I look up and give a start – I am outside Semb's again.

I quickly make a full turn, hiding the parcel in front of me, and hurry down Kirke Street, fearful and ashamed that someone might have seen me from the window. I pass Ingebret's and the theatre and, turning at the Lodge Building, head down towards the water and the Fortress. I find a bench again and start racking my brains afresh.

Where in the world was I to find shelter for tonight? Wasn't there a hole someplace where I could sneak in and hide until morning? My pride forbade me to return to my room, it would never occur to me to go back on my word. I rejected this idea with great indignation, smiling inwardly in disdain at the thought of the little red rocking chair. By an association of ideas I suddenly found myself in a big two-bay room I had lived in once in the Hægdehaugen section: I saw a tray on the table loaded with huge sandwiches, it changed and turned into a beefsteak, a seductive beefsteak, a snow-white napkin, bread galore, a silver fork. The door opened: my landlady came to offer me more tea. . . .

Visions and dreams! I told myself that if I took some food now, my head would be confused again, my brain would get feverish as before, and I would have lots of crazy ideas to contend with. I couldn't stand food, I wasn't made that way; it was a peculiarity of mine, an idiosyncrasy.

Perhaps something would turn up in the way of shelter later in the evening. There was no hurry; at worst I could take to the woods somewhere, I had the entire city environs to choose from and there was no frost in the air.

The sea out yonder swayed in a brooding repose. Ships and fat, broad-nosed barges ploughed trenches in its lead-coloured surface, scattering streaks left and right, and glided on, while the smoke rolled out of their funnels like downy quilts and the piston strokes came through with a muffled sound in the clammy air. There was no sun and no wind, the trees behind me were wet, and the bench I sat on was cold and damp. Time passed; I fell into a doze and grew sleepy, a slight chill creeping along my spine. A moment later I felt my eyelids begin to close. And I let them close. . . .

When I awoke it was dark all around; dazed and frozen, I jumped up, grabbed my parcel and started walking. I walked faster and faster to get warm, flapped my arms and rubbed my legs, which I could barely feel any more, and came up to the firehouse. It was nine o'clock; I had slept several hours.

Where was I to go? I had to be somewhere, after all. I stand there staring up at the firehouse, pondering whether I could manage to get into one of the hallways, watching out for a moment when the patrol turned his back. I climb the stairs ready to talk to the man, who immediately lifts his axe in salute and waits for what I'm going to say. This axe held high, its edge turned toward me, cuts through my nerves like a cold blow; I'm struck dumb with terror before this armed man and involuntarily pull back. I don't say a word, just slip further and further away from him; to save face I pass my hand over my forehead as though I had forgotten something and slink away. When I found myself on the pavement again, I felt saved, as if I had just escaped a great danger. And I hurried off.

Cold and hungry and more and more uneasy, I wandered up Karl Johan Street. I began cursing quite loudly and didn't care if someone could hear me. At the Storting, near the first lion, I suddenly remember, through a fresh association of ideas, a painter I knew, a young person I had once saved from getting slapped in the amusement park and had later visited. I snap my fingers and head for Tordenskjold Street, find a door with the name C. Zacharias Bartel on a card and knock.

He came to the door himself; he reeked something awful of beer and tobacco.

'Good evening,' I said.

'Good evening. Oh, it's you. Why the hell have you come so late? It doesn't really look good by lamplight. I've added a haystack since the last time you saw it and made a few alterations. You have to see it in the daytime, it's no use trying to do it now.'

'Let me see it anyway,' I said. Actually, I didn't remember which picture he was talking about.

'Absolutely impossible!' he replied. 'It would all look yellow. And then there's something else' – he came toward me, whispering – 'I have a little girl with me tonight, so it just can't be done.'

'Well, in that case it's out of the question, of course.'

I stepped back, said goodnight, and left.

Apparently there was no alternative but to go out into the woods somewhere. If only the ground hadn't been so damp! I patted my blanket and felt more and more reconciled to the idea of sleeping under the open sky. I had taken such pains, for such a long time, to find a lodging in town that I was sick and tired of the whole thing. It gave me a sweet sense of pleasure to take it easy, resign myself and drift along the street without a thought in my head. I dropped by the University clock and could see it was after ten, and from there I headed uptown. Someplace in the Hægdehaugen area I stopped outside a grocer's where some food was displayed in the window. A cat lay asleep beside a round loaf of white bread, and just behind it was a bowl of lard and several jars of oats. I stood eyeing these eatables a while, but since I didn't have anything to buy with I turned away from them and continued my tramp. I walked very slowly, passed Majorstuen, continued onward, always onward, walked for hours, and finally got out to the Bogstad Woods.

Here I stepped off the road and sat down to rest. Then I busied myself looking for a likely place, began to scrape together some heather and juniper twigs and made a bed on a small slope where it was fairly dry, opened my parcel and took out the blanket. I was tired and fagged out from the long walk and went to bed at once. I tossed and turned many times before I finally got settled; my ear hurt – it was a bit swollen from the blow of the fellow on the hay load and I couldn't lie on it. I took off my shoes and placed them under my head, with the big wrapping paper on top of them.

A brooding darkness was all around me. Everything was still, everything. But up aloft soughed the eternal song of wind and weather, that remote, tuneless hum which is never silent. I listened so long to this endless, faint soughing that it began to confuse me; it could only be the symphonies coming from the whirling worlds above me, the stars intoning a hymn. . . .

'Like hell it is!' I said, laughing aloud to buoy myself up. 'It is the night owls of Canaan hooting!'

I got up, lay down again, put on my shoes and wandered about in the dark, lay down afresh, fought and battled fear and anger until the early morning hours, when I finally fell asleep.

It was broad daylight when I opened my eyes, and I had a hunch it was almost noon. I pulled on my shoes, wrapped up my blanket and headed back to the city. There was no sun to be seen today either, and I was frozen stiff; my legs were dead and my eyes started watering as though they couldn't stand the daylight.

It was three o'clock. My hunger was getting rather bad, I felt faint and threw up a bit here and there on the sly. I took a turn down to the Steam Kitchen, read the items on the board and shrugged my shoulders conspicuously, as though salt meat and pork weren't food for me. From there I went on to Jærnbanetorvet Square.

Suddenly a curious confusion flashed through my head; I walked on, refusing to pay any attention to it, but it got worse and worse and finally I had to sit down on a doorstep. My mind was suffering a complete transformation, a tissue in my brain had snapped. I gasped for air a couple of times and remained sitting there, wondering. I was not insensible, being clearly aware of the slight pain in my ear from yesterday, and when an acquaintance came by I knew him at once, got up and bowed.

What sort of painful new sensation was this, coming on top of all the others? Was it a result of sleeping on the damp ground? Or was it due to the fact that I hadn't had breakfast yet? All in all, it was simply absurd to live like this. Holy Christ, what had I done to deserve this special persecution anyway! I simply couldn't understand. It struck me suddenly that I might as well turn myself into a crook right away and take the blanket to 'Uncle's' basement. I could pawn it for one krone in cash, get myself three decent meals and keep going until I thought of something else. I would put off Hans Pauli with a fib. I was already on my way to the basement but stopped in front of the entrance, shook my head doubtfully and turned around.

As I walked away I felt more and more pleased that I had conquered this great temptation. The consciousness of being honest went to my head, filling me with the glorious sensation that I was a man of character, a white beacon in the midst of a turbid human sea with floating wreckage everywhere. To hock someone else's property for a meal, to eat and drink and your soul be damned, to call yourself a crook to your face and hide from your own eyes – never! Never! The idea had never been in earnest, it had scarcely even occurred to me; you couldn't really be held responsible for your idle, fleeting thoughts by the way, especially when you had an awful headache and were nearly killing yourself lugging about a blanket that belonged to someone else.

Anyhow, something was bound to turn up in the way of help at the right time! There was that shopkeeper on Grønlandsleret, for example. Had I been pestering him every hour of the day since sending in my application? Had I rung his bell at all times and been turned away? I hadn't as much as reported back to him for his answer. It didn't have to be an entirely fruitless attempt, perhaps I had been lucky this time. Luck often followed such a strangely winding path. So I set out for Grønlandsleret Street.

The last shock that had passed through my brain had left me somewhat weak, and I walked extremely slowly, thinking about what I would say to the shopkeeper. Maybe he was a good soul; if he was in the right mood, he might even let me have a krone in advance without my asking. Such people were apt to come up with some really excellent ideas every now and then.

I sneaked into a doorway and blackened the knees of my trousers with spit so I'd look fairly respectable, left my blanket behind a box in a dark corner, crossed the street and stepped into the little store.

A man stands before me, busy pasting some bags together from old newspapers.

'I would like to see Mr Christie,' I said.

'That's me,' the man replied.

Well! My name was such and such, I had taken the liberty of sending him an application, and I was wondering if it had done me any good.

He repeated my name a couple of times and started laughing. 'Well, here you are,' he said, taking my letter from his breast pocket. 'Sir, take note, if you please, of the way you deal with figures. You have dated your letter 1848!' And the man roared with laughter.

'Yes, that's pretty bad,' I said, crestfallen – a slip, absent-mindedness, I admitted that.

'You see, I must have someone who won't ever make a mistake with figures,' he said. 'I'm very sorry – your handwriting is so clear, and I also like your letter otherwise, but . . .'

I waited a while; this couldn't possibly be the man's last word. He addressed himself to his bags again.

'Well, that's a shame,' I said, 'an awful shame, really.' But needless to say, it would never happen again, and this little slip of the pen couldn't have made me unfit for keeping books altogether, could it?

'No, I'm not saying that,' he replied, 'but still it carried so much weight with me that I decided in favour of someone else right away.'

'So the position is taken?' I asked.

'Yes.'

'Oh, dear! Well, there's nothing more to be done about that, is there?'

'No. I am sorry, but—'

'Goodbye,' I said.

A brutal, red-hot anger flared up in me. I fetched

my parcel in the entranceway, clenched my teeth, ran into peaceful folk on the pavement without apologising. When a gentleman stopped and reprimanded me sharply for my behaviour, I turned around and screamed a single meaningless word into his ear, shook my fists under his nose and walked on, appalled by a blind rage that I couldn't control. He called a policeman, and I could wish for nothing better than to get my hands on a policeman for a moment, so I slowed my pace on purpose to give him a chance to overtake me; but he didn't come. What sense could there possibly be to having absolutely all one's most sincere and diligent endeavours come to nothing? Why had I written 1848 anyway? What was that damned year to me? Here I was walking around so hungry that my intestines were squirming inside me like snakes, and I had no guarantee there would be something in the way of food later in the day either. And as time went on I was getting more and more hollowed out, spiritually and physically, and I stooped to less and less honourable actions every day. I lied without blushing to get my way, cheated poor people out of their rent, even had to fight off the thought, mean as could be, of laying hands on other people's blankets, all without remorse, without a bad conscience. Rotten patches were beginning to appear in my inner being, black spongy growths that were spreading more and more. And God sat up in his heaven keeping a watchful eye on me, making sure that my destruction took place according to all the rules of the game, slowly and steadily, with no let-up. But in the pit of hell the devils were raising their hackles in fury because it was taking me such a long time to commit a cardinal sin, an unforgivable sin for which God in his righteousness had to cast me down. . . .

I quickened my walk, forging ahead faster and faster, swung suddenly to the left and, excited and angry, stepped into a light, decorated entranceway. I didn't stop, not even for a second, but the entire curious décor of the entrance immediately penetrated my consciousness. As I ran up the stairs, the most insignificant details of the doors, the ornaments and the paving stood out clearly in my mind's eye. I furiously rang a bell on the second floor. Why did I stop exactly on the second floor? And why grab exactly this bell rope, which was the furthest from the stairway?

A young lady in a grey dress with black trimmings opened the door. She looked at me in amazement for a moment, then she shook her head and said, 'We don't have anything today.' And she made as though to close the door.

Why in the world had I gotten myself involved with this person? She took me for a beggar out of hand, and I suddenly became cold and calm. I took off my hat and made a respectful bow and, pretending I hadn't heard her words, said with extreme politeness, 'I beg your pardon, miss, for ringing so loudly, I wasn't familiar with the bell. There's supposed to be an ailing gentleman here who has advertised for someone to wheel him about in his carriage.'

She stood awhile turning this mendacious fancy over in her mind, and seemed to grow doubtful what to think of me.

'No,' she said at last, 'there is no ailing gentleman here.'

'Really? An elderly gentleman, a two hours' ride every day, at forty øre an hour?'

'No.'

'Then I beg your pardon again,' I said; 'maybe it was on the first floor. In any event, I just wanted to recommend a person of my acquaintance in whom I take an interest. My name is Wedel-Jarlsberg.' I bowed again and withdrew. The young lady turned flaming red; in her embarrassment she remained rooted to the spot, but followed me with an intent gaze as I descended the stairs.

My composure had returned and my head was clear. The lady's words to the effect that she had nothing to give me today had struck me like a cold shower. I had come to such a pass now that anybody could point at me mentally and say to herself: There goes a beggar, one of those who get their food handed to them through the front door!

On Møller Street I stopped outside a tavern and sniffed the fresh aroma of meat roasting inside; I had already put my hand on the doorknob and was about to go in to no purpose, but I thought better of it and walked away. When I got to Stortorvet Square and looked for a spot where I could rest a while, all the benches were taken, and I searched in vain all around the church for a quiet place where I could settle down. Of course! I said gloomily to myself, of course, of course! And I took to wandering again. I made a detour down to the drinking fountain at the corner of the Arcades and drank a mouthful of water, then went on, dragging myself forward step by step, taking time for long pauses in front of every shop window and stopping to follow every passing carriage with my eyes. I felt a white heat in my head, and my temples were pounding strangely. The water I had drunk disagreed very badly with me, and I vomited a bit here and there in the street. In this way I got as far as Christ's Cemetery. I sat down with my elbows on my knees and my head between my hands; in this curled-up position I was comfortable and no longer felt the gnawing pain in my chest.

A stonecutter lay on his stomach on top of a large granite slab beside me, cutting an inscription; he was wearing blue glasses and immediately reminded me of an acquaintance whom I had nearly forgotten, a man who worked in a bank and whom I had met some time ago in the Oplandske Café.

If only I could cast off all sense of shame and turn to him! Tell him the truth straight out – that I was getting to be rather strapped and had difficulty keeping body and soul together. I could give him my shaving book. . . . I'll be damned, my shaving book! Coupons for almost one krone! I reach nervously for this valuable treasure. When I don't find it fast enough, I jump up, search for it in a cold sweat, and find it finally at the bottom of my breast pocket together with other papers, blank and filled with writing, worthless. I count these six coupons many times, forward and backward; I didn't really need them very much, it could be taken as a caprice on my part, a whimsical notion that I didn't feel like shaving any more. I was tided over by half a krone, a white half-krone in silver from the Kongsberg mint! The bank closed at six, I could be on the lookout for my man outside the Oplandske Café around seven or eight.

I sat there rejoicing in this thought for quite a while.

Time was passing, the wind was blowing hard in the chestnut trees around me, and the day was coming to an end. But wasn't it a bit cheap to come and sneak six shaving coupons into the hands of a young gentleman who worked in a bank? For all I knew, he might have two chock-full shaving books in his pocket, with coupons that were far, far nicer and cleaner than mine. I felt in all my pockets for some more things which I could throw in with them, but found none. What if I offered him my tie? I could easily do without as long as I buttoned my coat up tight, which I had to do anyway since I no longer had a vest. I undid it, a big cravat-type bow tie that covered half my chest, brushed it carefully, and wrapped it in a piece of white writing paper together with the shaving book. Then I left the cemetery and went down to the Oplandske Café.

The clock on the city jail showed seven. I hovered around the café, shuffling up and down along the iron railing and keeping a sharp lookout for all who came and went. Finally, at about eight o'clock, I saw the young man, fresh and elegant, coming up the hill and cutting across towards the café entrance. The moment I caught sight of him my heart ran riot in my breast like a caged bird, and I came straight to the point, without even saying hello.

'A half-krone, my old friend!' I said, making myself bold. 'Here – here's value for your money.' And I stuck the little packet into his hand.

'Haven't got it,' he said, 'I swear to God!' And he turned his purse inside out under my very eyes. 'I was out last night and went bust. You must believe me, I haven't got it.'

'Of course, my friend, I understand,' I answered, taking his word for it. There was no reason, after all, why he should lie in such a small matter; in fact, his blue eyes seemed all but moist when he examined his pockets and didn't find anything. I turned back. 'Please excuse me, then,' I said. 'I just happen to be in a tight spot right now.'

I was already some distance down the street when he called after me about the packet.

'Keep it, just keep it!' I replied. 'You are quite welcome to it. It's only a couple of small things, nothing really – pretty much all my possessions on this earth.' I was moved by my own words – they sounded so dismal in the evening twilight – and burst into tears.

The wind was blowing more briskly, the clouds scudded furiously across the sky, and it became chillier and chillier as it grew dark. Walking down the street I cried without a break, feeling more and more sorry for myself, and time after time I repeated a few words, an exclamation which drew fresh tears when they were about to stop: 'Oh God, I'm so miserable! Oh God, I'm so miserable!'

An hour passed – it passed exceedingly slowly and sluggishly. I hung about on Torv Street a while, sat on the steps, slipped into the entranceways when someone came by, or stood staring vacuously into the illuminated little shops where people were scurrying about with merchandise and money. At last I found myself a snug spot behind a lumber pile between the church and the Arcades.

No, I couldn't go out to the woods tonight, no matter what; I didn't have the strength for it and it was so endlessly far away. I would stay where I was and get through the night as best I could. If it became too cold I could stroll about a bit by the church, I didn't intend to make any more fuss about that. I leaned back and drowsed.

The noise around me diminished, the stores closed, the footsteps of the pedestrians were heard more and more seldom, and eventually the lights went out in the windows. . . .

Opening my eyes, I noticed a figure in front of me; the shiny buttons that gleamed toward me made me suspect a policeman. I couldn't see the man's face.

'Good evening,' he said.

'Good evening,' I answered, feeling scared. I got up, embarrassed. He stood motionless a while.

'Where do you live?' he asked.

By force of habit, and without reflecting, I named my old address, the little attic room I had given up.

He stood a while again.

'Have I done something wrong?' I asked fearfully.

'No, not at all,' he answered. 'But you ought to go home now, don't you think, it's cold lying here.'

'Yes, it's chilly, I can feel it.'

I said goodnight and instinctively set out for my old place. If I watched my step I was pretty sure I could walk up without being heard – there were eight flights of stairs in all, and only the two top ones had creaky steps.

I took off my shoes in the entrance and went up. It was quiet everywhere. On the second floor I heard the slow tick-tock of a clock and a child crying softly; then I heard nothing more. I found my door, lifted it slightly on its hinges and opened it without a key as I was used to doing, entered the room and pulled the door shut without a sound.

Everything was just as I had left it – the curtains were pulled away from the windows and the bed was empty. Over on the table I glimpsed a piece of paper, probably my note to the landlady. So she hadn't even been up here since I went away. I fumbled with my hand over the white spot and felt to my surprise that it was a letter. A letter? I take it over to the window, scan the badly written characters as best I can in the dark, and finally make out my own name. Aha! I think, the landlady's answer, warning me not to set foot in the room any more in case I should wish to come back!

And slowly, quite slowly, I walk out of the room again, carrying my shoes in one hand, the letter in the other, and the blanket under my arm. Clenching my teeth, I tread lightly on the creaky steps, make it safely down all those flights of stairs, and find myself in the entranceway once more.

I put on my shoes again, taking my time with the laces; I even sit still for a moment after I've finished, staring blankly ahead of me and holding the letter in my hand.

Then I stand up and leave.

The flickering light of a street lamp twinkles up the street, so I walk right under the light, lean my parcel up against the lamppost and open the letter, doing it all with extreme slowness.

A stream of light seems to surge through my breast, and I hear myself giving a little cry, a meaningless sound of joy: the letter was from the editor, my story was accepted, it had gone directly to the composing room! 'A few minor changes . . . corrected a few slips of the pen . . . promising work . . . to be printed tomorrow . . . ten kroner.'

Laughing and crying, I made a running start and raced down the street, stopped to slap my thighs and flung a solemn oath into space for no particular reason. And time passed.

All night long, till daybreak, I went yodelling about the streets dazed with joy, repeating: promising work, meaning a little masterpiece, a stroke of genius. And ten kroner!

Part Two

A couple of weeks later I found myself outdoors one night.

I had once again been sitting in one of the cemeteries working on an article for one of the papers. While I was busy with this it got to be ten o'clock, darkness came on, and the gate was going to be closed. I was hungry, very hungry; those ten kroner, I'm sorry to say, were gone all too quickly. It was now two, nearly three, days since I had eaten anything and I felt weak, slightly fatigued from moving my pencil. I had a half-penknife and a bunch of keys in my pocket, but not a penny.

When the cemetery gate closed I should have gone straight home, but from an instinctive fear of my completely dark and empty room – an abandoned tinsmith's shop where I had finally been allowed to stay for the time being – I shambled on, wandering aimlessly past the city jail, all the way down to the harbour and over to a bench on Jærnbane Pier, where I sat down.

At that moment not a single sad thought entered my mind; I forgot my privation and felt soothed by the sight of the harbour, which lay there lovely and peaceful in the semi-darkness. By force of habit I wanted to give myself the treat of skimming through the piece I had just written, which seemed to my aching brain the best thing I had ever done. I pulled the manuscript out of my pocket, held it up close in order to see, and browsed through one page after another. In the end I got tired and put the papers back in my pocket. Everything was still; the sea stretched away like blue mother-of-pearl, and small birds flew silently by from one place to another. A policeman is patrolling his beat some distance off, otherwise there is not a soul to be seen and the entire harbour is quiet.

I count my money again: a half-penknife, a bunch of keys, but not a penny. Suddenly I dip into my pocket and pull out my papers once more. It was a mechanical action, an unconscious twitch of the nerves. I picked a white, blank page and – God only knows where I got the idea from – made a cone, closed it carefully to make it look full and threw it along the pavement, far out. It was carried yet a bit further by the wind, then lay still.

By this time hunger had begun to attack me. I sat eyeing that white cornet, which looked as though swollen with shiny silver coins, and worked myself up to believing that it really did contain something. I kept cajoling myself, aloud, into guessing the amount – if I guessed correctly it was mine! I imagined the nice little ten-øre coins at the bottom and the fat, milled krone pieces on top – a whole cornet chock-full of money! My eyes popping, I sat there staring at it, egging myself on to go and steal it.

Then I hear the officer cough. What put it into my head to do exactly the same? I get up from the bench and cough, repeating the cough three times to catch his ear. How he would pounce on that cornet when he came! I sat there rejoicing over this trick, rubbing my hands with delight and rapping out grand curses at random. Wouldn't he end up laughing on the wrong side of his mouth though, the dog! Wouldn't he just sink into the bottomless pit and fry in hell for this dirty trick! I was drunk with starvation, my hunger had made me intoxicated.

A few minutes later the policeman comes along, rapping his iron heels on the paving stones and peering on all sides. He takes his time, having the whole night before him; he doesn't see the cornet, not until he's quite close to it. Then he stops and gazes at it. It looks so white and precious lying there, perhaps a tidy little sum, eh? A tidy little sum of silver coins? . . . He picks it up. Hmm! It's light, very light. Maybe an expensive plume, hat trim. . . . He opens it carefully with his big hands and peeps inside. I laughed, laughed and slapped my knees, laughed like a madman. And not a sound emerged from my throat; my laughter was feverish and silent, with the intensity of tears. . . .

Then there is again the clitter-clatter on the cobblestones, and the officer takes a turn along the pier. I sat there with tears in my eyes, gasping for breath, quite beside myself with feverish merriment. I began to talk aloud, told myself the story of the cornet, aped the poor policeman's movements, peeped into the hollow of my hand and repeated over and over to myself: He coughed when he threw it away! He coughed when he threw it away! I added new words, with titillating supplements, changed the whole sentence and made it more pointed: He coughed once – huh-huh!

I spent myself in variations on these words, and it got to be late evening before my merriment ceased. Then a drowsy calm came over me, a pleasant fatigue which I did nothing to resist. The darkness had become thicker now, and a light breeze ruffled the mother-of-pearl of the sea. The ships whose masts I saw outlined against the sky looked, with their black hulls, like silent monsters that were raising their hackles and lying in wait for me. I suffered no pain, my hunger had taken the edge off; instead I felt pleasantly empty, untouched by everything around me and happy to be unseen by all. I put my legs up on the bench and leaned back, the best way to feel the true well-being of seclusion. There wasn't a cloud in my mind, nor did I feel any discomfort, and I hadn't a single unfulfilled desire or craving as far as my thoughts could reach. I lay with open eyes in a state of utter absence from myself and felt deliciously out of it.

So far not a sound disturbed me; the soft darkness had hidden the whole world from my sight and buried me in sheer quietude – only the desolate, muted voice of stillness whispers monotonously in my ear. The dark monsters out there would suck me up when night came on, and they would carry me far across the sea and through strange lands where no humans lived. They would bring me to Princess Ylajali's castle, where an undreamed-of splendour awaited me, exceeding that of all others. And she herself will be sitting in a sparkling hall where all is of amethyst, on a throne of yellow roses, and she will hold out her hand to me when I enter, greet me and bid me welcome as I approach and kneel down: Welcome, my knight, to me and my land! I've waited twenty summers for you and summoned you on every white night; and when you grieved I wept in this room, and when you slept I breathed lovely dreams into you. . . . And the fair one takes my hand and pulls me along, leads me through long corridors where big crowds of people shout hurrahs, through bright gardens where three hundred young damsels are playing games and laughing, and into another hall where all is of brilliant emerald. Here the sun shines, beguiling choral music floats through the galleries and corridors, and waves of fragrance waft toward me. I hold her hand in mine and feel the wild beauty of enchantment race through my blood; I put my arm around her and she whispers, Not here, come further still! And we enter the red hall where all is of rubies, a foaming splendour in which I swoon. Then I feel her arms around me, she breathes upon my face and whispers, Welcome, my love! Kiss me! Again . . . again . . .

From my bench I see stars before my eyes, and my thoughts are swept up into a hurricane of light. . . .

I had fallen asleep where I lay and was awakened by the policeman. There I was, mercilessly called back to life and my misery. My first feeling was a stupid amazement at finding myself out in the open, but this was soon replaced by a bitter despondency; I was on the verge of crying with grief at still being alive. It had rained while I slept, my clothes were soaking wet, and I felt a raw chill in my limbs. The darkness had become even thicker, I could barely make out the officer's features in front of me.

'Stand up now, will you!' he said.

I got up immediately; if he had ordered me to lie down

again, I would also have obeyed. I was very depressed and quite weak, and besides I started almost instantly to feel the pangs of hunger again.

'Wait a minute, you idiot!' the officer called after me. 'You're walking off without your hat. There, now go on!'

'It seemed to me too there was something – something I had forgotten,' I stammered absent-mindedly. 'Thanks. Goodnight.'

And I shambled off.

If only one had a piece of bread! One of those delicious little loaves of rye bread that you could munch on as you walked the streets. And I kept picturing to myself just the sort of rye bread it would have been good to have. I was bitterly hungry, wished myself dead and gone, grew sentimental and cried. There would never be an end to my misery! Then I stopped suddenly in the street, stamped my feet on the cobblestones and swore aloud. What was it he had called me? Fool? I'd show that policeman what it meant to call me a fool! With that I turned around and rushed back. I felt flaming hot with anger. Some way down the street I stumbled and fell, but I took no notice, jumped up again and ran on. On reaching Jærnbanetorvet Square, however, I was so tired that I didn't feel up to going all the way to the pier; besides, my anger had cooled off during the run. Finally I stopped to catch my breath. Who gave a hoot what such a policeman had said? – All right, but I wasn't going to swallow everything! – True enough! I interrupted myself, but he didn't know any better. I found this excuse to be satisfactory; I repeated to myself that he didn't know any better. And so I turned around once more.

God, the sort of ideas you get! I thought angrily: running around like a madman on sopping-wet streets in the dead of night! My hunger pains were excruciating and didn't leave me for a moment. I swallowed my saliva again and again to take the edge off, and it seemed to help. I hadn't had enough to eat for many, many weeks before this thing came up, and my strength had diminished considerably lately. When I had been lucky enough to get my hands on a five-krone bill by some manoeuvre or other, the money generally didn't last me long enough for my health to be fully restored before a new hunger spell descended upon me. My back and shoulders had borne the brunt of it; I could stop that gnawing pain in my chest for a moment by coughing hard or by walking extremely bent over, but there was nothing I could do for my back and shoulders. Anyway, why did my prospects simply refuse to brighten up? Didn't I have the same right to life as anyone else, like Pascha the second-hand bookdealer, or Hennechen the steamship agent? Didn't I have the shoulders of a giant and two stout arms for work, and hadn't I even applied for a job as a woodcutter on Møller Street to earn my daily bread? Was I lazy? Hadn't I applied for work and listened to lectures and written newspaper articles and read and slogged away like mad day and night? And hadn't I lived like a miser, eaten bread and milk when I had plenty, bread when I had little, and gone hungry when I had nothing? Did I live in a hotel, did I have a suite on the ground floor? I lived in a godforsaken loft, a tinsmith's shop abandoned by everybody and his brother last winter because it snowed in there. So I couldn't make head nor tail of the whole situation.

I was thinking about all this as I walked along, and there wasn't as much as a spark of malice, envy or bitterness in my thoughts.

I stopped outside a paint shop and looked in through the window; I tried to read the labels on a couple of tin cans, but it was too dark. Annoyed with myself for this new whim and stirred up and angry because I couldn't find out what was in those cans, I knocked once on the window and walked on. Seeing a police officer up the street, I quickened my pace, went right up to him and said, without a shadow of a pretext, 'It's ten o'clock.'

'No, it's two,' he answered, surprised.

'No, it's ten,' I said. 'It's ten o'clock.' And, groaning with anger, I took another couple of steps forward, clenched my fist and said, 'Listen, you know what — it's ten o'clock.'

He pondered a while, giving me the once-over and staring at me in bewilderment. At last he said, rather quietly, 'It's time for you to go home in any case, isn't it? Would you like me to come with you?'

I was disarmed by this show of friendliness; I felt the tears coming and hastened to answer, 'No, thanks! I have only been to a café and it got a bit late. Thank you very much all the same.'

He touched his helmet for goodbye as I left. His friendliness had overwhelmed me, and I cried because I didn't have five kroner to give him. I stopped and followed him with my eyes as he slowly walked away, clapped my hand to my forehead and cried more and more desperately the further he got. I reviled myself for my poverty, shouted epithets at myself, invented insulting names, priceless treasures of coarse abusive language that I heaped on myself. I kept this up until I was nearly home. When I got to the gate I discovered I had lost my keys.

Of course, I said bitterly to myself, why shouldn't I lose my keys? Here I am, living in a house where there is a stable downstairs and a tinsmith's shop upstairs; the gate is locked at night, and no one – no one – can open it, so why shouldn't I lose my keys? I was as wet as a drowned rat, a bit hungry, just a wee bit hungry, and ridiculously tired in the knees, just a little – so why shouldn't I lose them? For that matter, why couldn't the whole house have been moved out to Aker township when I got home and wanted to go in? . . . And I laughed to myself, hardened by hunger and exhaustion.

I heard the horses stomping their feet in the stable and could see my window upstairs, but I couldn't open the gate and get in. And so, tired and bitter at heart, I decided to go back to the pier and look for my keys.

It had started to rain again and I could already feel the water soaking through on my shoulders. At the jail I suddenly had a bright idea: I would ask the police to open their gate. I turned to an officer at once and begged him earnestly to come and let me in, if he could.

Yes, of course, if he could! But he couldn't, he didn't have a key. The police keys weren't here, they were in the detective department.

What was I to do then?

Well, I had better go to a hotel and turn in.

But I really couldn't go to a hotel and turn in, I didn't have any money. I had been out, in a café, he would surely understand . . .

We stood a little while on the steps of the jail. He considered and pondered and looked me up and down. Just beyond us the rain was pouring.

'Then you'd better go to the officer on duty and report yourself as homeless,' he said.

As homeless! I hadn't thought of that. That was a damn good idea! I thanked the policeman on the spot for this excellent suggestion. All there was to it was to go in and say that I was homeless?

Yes, that was all! . . .

'Name?' the officer on duty asked.

'Tangen – Andreas Tangen.'

I don't know why I lied. My thoughts fluttered about in disarray and gave me more fanciful notions than I could handle. I hit upon this far-fetched name on the spur of the moment and tossed it out without any ulterior motive. I lied unnecessarily.

'Occupation?'

Now he was forcing me to the wall. Hmm! I thought first of turning myself into a tinsmith but didn't dare; I had given myself a name not borne by each and every tinsmith, and besides I was wearing glasses. Then it came into my head to be foolhardy – I took a step forward and said, firmly and solemnly, 'Journalist.'

The officer on duty gave a start before writing it down, and I stood before the counter with the lofty air of a homeless cabinet minister. It didn't arouse any suspicion; the officer could understand quite well why

I had hesitated with my answer. Had anyone heard the like, a journalist in jail, without a roof over his head!

'With which paper, Mr Tangen?'

'With *Morgenbladet*,' I said. 'I'm afraid I've been out a bit late this evening—'

'Well, we won't mention that,' he broke in, adding with a smile, 'when youth steps out, you know . . . We understand!' Turning to an officer he said, as he rose and bowed politely to me, 'Show this gentleman up to the reserved section. Goodnight.'

I felt the chills running down my spine at my boldness, and I clenched my hands as I followed him, to stay tough.

'The gas light will be on for ten minutes,' the officer said from the doorway.

'And then it goes out?'

'Then it goes out.'

I sat down on the bed and heard the key being turned. The bright cell looked friendly; I felt safely indoors and listened with pleasure to the rain outside. How could I wish for anything better than such an excellent cell! My feeling of contentment grew; sitting on the bed, hat in hand and my eyes fixed upon the gas jet on the wall, I started to mull over the high points of my first involvement with the police. This was the first time, and how I had fooled them! Journalist Tangen, beg your pardon? And then *Morgenbladet*! I had really struck home with *Morgenbladet*! We won't mention that, eh? Sat at the Prime Minister's dressed to the nines till two o'clock, forgot my gate key and a wallet with several thousand at home! Show that gentleman up to the reserved section. . . .

All of a sudden the gas goes out, so strangely all of a sudden, without diminishing, without dwindling; I sit in utter darkness, unable to see my own hand or the white walls around me – nothing. I had no choice but to go to bed. I got undressed.

But I wasn't sleepy and couldn't fall asleep. I lay a while looking into the darkness, a thick massive darkness without end that I wasn't able to fathom. My thoughts couldn't grasp it. It struck me as excessively dark and I felt its presence as oppressive. I closed my eyes, began to sing in an undertone, and tossed back and forth in the bunk to distract myself, but it was no use. The darkness had taken possession of my thoughts and didn't leave me alone for a moment. What if I myself were to be dissolved into darkness, made one with it? I sit up in bed and flail my arms.

My nervous state had got out of hand, and however hard I tried to fight it, it was no use. A prey to the quirkiest fantasies, there I sat shushing myself, humming lullabies, perspiring with the effort to calm myself down. I stared out into the darkness – and never in my born days had I seen such a darkness. There was no doubt that here I found myself before a special kind of darkness, a desperate element which no one had previously been aware of. The most ludicrous ideas filled my mind, and every little thing frightened me. I am greatly absorbed by the tiny hole in the wall by my bed, a nail hole I come across, a mark in the masonry. I feel it, blow into it, and try to guess its depth. That was no innocent hole, not by any means; it was a very intricate and mysterious hole that I had to beware of. Obsessed by the thought of this hole, quite beside myself with curiosity and fear, I finally had to get out of bed and find my half-penknife to measure its depth, so I could assure myself that it didn't go all the way into the next cell.

I lay back to try and fall asleep, but in reality to fight the darkness once more. The rain had stopped outside and I couldn't hear a sound. I kept listening for footsteps in the street for a while, and I didn't rest easy until I had heard a pedestrian go by, a policeman judging by the sound. Suddenly I snap my fingers several times and laugh. What the hell was this! Ha! I imagined I had found a new word. I sit up in bed and say, It doesn't exist in the language, I have invented it – *Kuboaa*. It does have letters like a word – Christ, man, you have invented a word. . . . *Kuboaa* . . . of great grammatical importance.

The word stood out sharply against the darkness before me.

I sit with open eyes, amazed at my find and laughing for joy. Then I start whispering: they might be spying on me, and I intended to keep my invention a secret. I had passed over into the sheer madness of hunger; I was empty and without pain and my thoughts were running riot. I debate with myself in silence. With the oddest jumps in my line of thought, I try to ascertain the meaning of my new word. It didn't have to mean either God or amusement park, and who had said it should mean cattle show? I clench my fist angrily and repeat once more, Who said that it shall mean cattle show? All things considered, it wasn't even necessary that it should mean padlock or sunrise. It wasn't difficult to make sense of such a word. I would wait and see. Meanwhile I would sleep on it.

I lie there on the bunk chuckling, but I don't say anything, express no opinion one way or the other. A few minutes go by and I get nervous, the new word worries me incessantly and keeps coming back; in the end it takes possession of all my thoughts and makes me stop laughing. I had made up my mind what the word shouldn't mean, but had taken no decision on what it should mean. That is a minor question! I said aloud to myself, clutching my arm and repeating that it was a minor question. The word had been found, thank God, and that was the main thing. But my thoughts worry me ceaselessly and keep me from falling asleep; nothing seemed to me good enough for this rare word. Finally I sit up in bed again, clasp my head with both hands and say, No, that's just what is impossible, letting it mean emigration or tobacco factory! If it could mean something like that, I would have decided in its favour long ago and taken the consequences. No, the word was really suited to mean something *spiritual*, a feeling, a state of mind – couldn't I understand that? And I try to jog my memory to come up with something spiritual. Then it seems to me that someone is speaking, sticking his nose into my chat, and I answer angrily, What was that? Oh my, you'll get the prize for biggest idiot! Knitting yarn? Go to hell! Why should I be under an obligation to let it mean knitting yarn when I was particularly opposed to its meaning knitting yarn? I had invented the word myself, and I was perfectly within my rights in having it mean anything whatsoever, for that matter. As far as I knew, I hadn't yet expressed an opinion. . . .

But my brain grew more and more perplexed. At last I

jumped out of bed to find the water tap. I wasn't thirsty, but my head was feverish and I felt instinctively a need for water. When I had had my drink, I went back to bed again and decided that I was going to sleep, by hook or by crook. I closed my eyes and forced myself to be quiet. I lay for several minutes without moving a muscle, began to sweat and felt the blood pulse violently through my veins. Wasn't it just too funny, though, that he should look for money in the cornet! And he coughed, just once. Is he still walking around down there? Sitting on my bench? . . . The blue mother-of-pearl . . . the ships . . .

I opened my eyes. How could I keep them closed anyway, when I wasn't able to sleep! The same brooding darkness around me, the same unfathomable black eternity which my thoughts recoiled from and couldn't grasp. What could I compare it to? I made the most desperate efforts to find a word black enough to signify this darkness for me, a word so horribly black that it would dirty my mouth when I uttered it. Good God, how dark it was! I am again put in mind of the harbour, the ships, those black monsters which lay waiting for me. They wanted to suck me up and hold me tight and sail with me by sea and land, through dark kingdoms no humans had ever seen. I can feel myself on board, pulled out to sea, soaring in the clouds, descending, descending. . . . I give a hoarse scream of terror and clutch the bed; I had been on such a perilous journey, had whizzed down through space like a switch. How wonderful it was to feel saved as I clapped my hand against that hard bunk bed! This is what it's like to die, I said to myself, and now you're going to die! I lay thinking about this, that now I was going to die, for a few moments. Then I sit up in bed and ask sternly, 'Who said I was going to die? Having found the word myself, I have the right to decide what it shall mean. . . .' I could hear that I was raving, could hear it even as I spoke. My madness was a delirium of weakness and exhaustion, but I was not out of my senses. All at once the thought flashed through my brain that I had gone mad. Terror-struck, I jump out of bed. I stagger over to the door, which I try to open, hurl myself against it a couple of times to force it, bang my head against the wall, groan aloud, bite my fingers, sob and curse. . . .

All was quiet, only my own voice echoed back from the walls. I had fallen on the floor, no longer able to stagger about in the cell. Then I glimpse high up, right in front of my eyes, a greyish square in the wall, a whitish tone, a hint of something – it was the daylight. Ah, what a delicious sigh of relief I gave! I threw myself flat on the floor and wept with joy over this blessed glimpse of light, sobbed out of gratitude, threw a kiss towards the window and behaved like a lunatic. At this moment, too, I was conscious of what I did. All despondency was gone immediately, all pain and despair had ceased, and I didn't have a single unfulfilled wish right then, as far as my thoughts could reach. I sat up on the floor, folded my hands, and waited patiently for daybreak.

What a night it had been! Strange, I thought with surprise, that they hadn't heard any noise. But then I was in the reserved section, high above all the prisoners. A homeless cabinet minister, if I might say so. Still in the best of moods, my eyes turned towards the ever-lightening window in the wall, I amused myself by acting the cabinet minister, calling myself Von Tangen and affecting a bureaucratic style. My fantasies had not ceased, I was only much less nervous. If only I hadn't made the deplorable slip of leaving my wallet at home! Might I have the honour of assisting the cabinet minister to bed? And in dead earnest, with much ceremony, I went over to the bunk and lay down.

It was now light enough to enable me to make out the contours of the cell fairly well, and a little later I could see the big door handle. This distracted my thoughts; the monotonous darkness, so exasperatingly thick that it had prevented me from seeing myself, was broken. Soon my blood grew quieter, and shortly I felt my eyes close.

I was awakened by a couple of raps on my door. I jumped up hastily and dressed in a hurry; my clothes were still soaking wet from last night.

'You will report downstairs to the guard on duty,' the officer said.

So I would have to suffer through fresh formalities, I thought, afraid.

I entered a big room downstairs where thirty or forty people were sitting, all homeless. One by one their names were called from the register, one by one they were given a meal ticket. The guard on duty was constantly saying to the officer by his side, 'Did he get a ticket? Don't forget to give them tickets. They look as though they could do with a meal.'

I was eyeing those tickets and wanted one for myself.

'Andreas Tangen, journalist!'

I stepped forward and bowed.

'Oh dear, how did *you* get here?'

I explained it all to him, giving the same story as last night; I told barefaced lies without blinking, lied with sincerity: Had been out a bit late, I was afraid, in a café, lost my gate key . . .

'Well,' he said and smiled, 'that's how it goes. Anyway, did you sleep well?'

'Like a cabinet minister!' I replied. 'Like a cabinet minister!'

'I'm pleased!' he said and stood up. 'Goodbye.'

And I left.

A ticket, a ticket for me too! I haven't eaten for more than three long days and nights. A loaf of bread! But nobody offered me a ticket and I didn't dare request one. That would have aroused instant suspicion. They would begin to poke around in my private affairs and find out who I really was; they would arrest me for making false pretences. – Head high, with the bearing of a millionaire and my hands gripping my lapels, I stride out of the jail.

The sun shone warmly by now, it was ten o'clock and the traffic at Youngstorvet Square was in full swing. Where was I to go? I pat my pocket to feel my manuscript; come eleven I would try to see the editor. I stand a while by the balustrade observing the activity below me; meanwhile my clothes had started steaming. Hunger again announced itself, gnawing and tugging at my chest and giving me small, sharp twinges of pain. Didn't I have a single friend, an acquaintance I could turn to? I search my memory for a man good for ten øre and can't find him. But what a beautiful day it was, with plenty of sun and light all around me; the sky flowed like a lovely ocean along the Lier mountains. . . .

Without knowing it, I was on my way home.

I was terribly hungry and picked up a wood chip in the street to chew on. It helped. Why hadn't I thought of that before!

The gate was open, the stableboy wished me good morning as usual.

'Nice weather!' he said.

'Yes,' I answered. That was all I could think of to say. Could I ask him to lend me a krone? He would probably be glad to if he could. Besides, I had written a letter for him once.

He stood there trying out something on his tongue, something he wanted to say.

'Yeah, nice weather. Hmm. I'm supposed to pay my landlady today. You wouldn't be so kind as to lend me five kroner, would you? Just for a few days. You helped me out once before, remember.'

'No, I really can't, Jens Olai,' I answered. 'Not now. Maybe later, this afternoon perhaps.' And I staggered up the stairs to my room.

I threw myself on my bed and laughed. What a lucky dog I was to have him steal a march on me! My honour was saved. Five kroner – good grief, man! You could just as well have asked me for five shares in the Steam Kitchen or for an estate out in Aker township.

The thought of those five kroner made me laugh louder and louder. Wasn't I a hell of a fellow though, eh? Five kroner! Of course, here was the right man! My mirth kept rising and I gave myself up to it: Damn it all, what a smell of cooking around here! A kitchen-fresh smell of meat patties from lunch time, ugh! And I push open the window to let this disgusting smell out. Waiter, a steak, please! Facing the table, this rickety table I had to support with my knees when writing, I bowed deeply and asked, Pardon me, but would you like a glass of wine? No? My name is Tangen, Cabinet Minister Tangen. Unfortunately I've been out a bit late . . . the gate key . . .

My thoughts were again running riot, racing along trackless paths. I was conscious all along that I was talking incoherently, and I didn't say a single word without hearing and understanding it. I said to myself, Now you're talking incoherently again! Still, I couldn't help it. It was like talking in your sleep while being awake. My head was light, without pain and without pressure, and my mind was without a cloud. I sailed off, putting up no resistance.

Come in! Yes, just come in! As you can see, all of rubies. Ylajali! Ylajali! The red, fluffy silk divan! How heavily she's breathing! Kiss me, my love – again, again. Your arms are like amber, your lips are flaming red. . . . Waiter, I ordered a steak. . . .

The sun shone in through my window, downstairs I could hear the horses chomping their oats. I sat munching on my wood chip, in high spirits, happy as a child. I had been continually groping for my manuscript; it wasn't even in my thoughts, but my instinct told me it was there, my blood reminded me of it. I pulled it out.

It had gotten wet, and I spread it out and placed it in the sun. Then I began to pace back and forth in my room. How depressing everything looked! Small tin shavings scattered all over the floor, but not a chair to sit in, not even a nail in the bare walls. It had all gone to 'Uncle's' cellar and been consumed. A few sheets of paper on the table, coated with a thick layer of dust, were my sole possessions; that old green blanket on the bed had been lent to me by Hans Pauli some months ago. . . . Hans Pauli! I snap my fingers. Hans Pauli Pettersen will help me out! I try to recall his address. How could I have forgotten Hans Pauli! He was bound to be very hurt that I hadn't come to him right away. I quickly don my hat, gather up the manuscript and hurry down the stairs.

'Listen, Jens Olai,' I call into the stable. 'I'm pretty sure I'll have something for you this afternoon.'

On reaching the jail, I can see it's past eleven, and I decide to drop in at the editor's then and there. I stopped outside the door to the office to check if my pages were in the right order; I smoothed them carefully out, stuck them back in my pocket and knocked. My heart beat audibly as I entered.

Scissors is there as usual. I ask timidly for the editor. No answer. The man sits there with a pair of long scissors digging up small news items in the provincial papers.

I repeat my question and step closer.

'The editor hasn't come in yet,' Scissors said finally, without looking up.

When would he be there?

Couldn't say, couldn't say at all.

How late would the office be open?

To this I got no answer, and I had to leave. Scissors hadn't glanced at me throughout; he had heard my voice and recognised me by that. This is how unwelcome you are here, I thought, they don't even bother to answer you. I wonder if it is by order of the editor. True enough, from the very moment my famous story at ten kroner was accepted, I had flooded him with manuscripts, pestering him almost every day with useless things he'd had to read and return to me. Perhaps he wanted to put an end to it, take his precautions. . . . I set out for the Homansbyen section.

Hans Pauli Pettersen was a peasant student living in the attic of a five-storey building, and so Hans Pauli Pettersen was a poor man. But if he had a krone he didn't begrudge it. I would get it as surely as if I already held it in my hand. Every minute of the way, I was looking forward to having this krone, and I felt certain I would get it. When I reached the front door it was locked, and I had to ring the bell.

'I'm here to see Pettersen, the student,' I said, about to enter. 'I know where his room is.'

'Pettersen, the student?' the maid repeats. Was it the one who used to live in the attic? He had moved. She didn't know where, but he had asked that his letters be sent down to Hermansen on Toldbod Street, and the maid gave me the number.

I walk, full of hope and faith, all the way down to Toldbod Street to ask about Hans Pauli's address. This was my last resort, and I had to use it. On the way I passed a newly-built house, in front of which a couple of carpenters were planing. I picked a few shiny shavings from the pile, stuck one in my mouth and put the other away in my pocket for later. I kept on going. I groaned from hunger. I had seen a fabulously big ten-øre loaf in the window of a bakery, the biggest loaf of bread that could be had for that price. . . .

'I'm here to find out the address of Mr Pettersen, the student.'

'Bernt Anker Street, number 10, the attic.' Was I going out there? Oh, then perhaps I would be kind enough to take along a couple of letters that had come for him?

Once more I walk uptown, the same way I had come, again I pass the carpenters, now sitting with their tin pails between their knees eating their good, warm Steam Kitchen meal, go past the bakery, where the loaf of bread is still in its place, and at last reach Bernt Anker Street half-dead with exhaustion. The door is open, and I start up all those trying flights of stairs to the attic. I take the letters from my pocket, to put Hans Pauli in a good mood at one blow when I entered. He surely wouldn't refuse me a helping hand when I explained my situation to him, oh no; Hans Pauli had such a big heart, I'd always said that about him.

I found his card on the door. 'H. P. Pettersen, stud. theol. – gone home.'

I sat down instantly, sat on the bare floor, dog-tired, undone by prostration. I repeat mechanically a couple of times, Gone home! Gone home! Then I keep perfectly still. There wasn't a tear in my eyes, I had neither thoughts nor feelings of any kind. I sat staring at the letters with wide-open eyes without doing a thing. Ten minutes went by, perhaps twenty or more, and I still sat there on the same spot, not moving a finger. This dull stupor was almost like a nap. Then I hear someone coming up the stairs and I get up and say, 'I'm looking for Mr Pettersen, the student – I have two letters for him.'

'He's gone home,' the woman answers. 'But he'll be back after the vacation. I could take the letters, of course, if you like.'

'Thanks, that's nice of you,' I said, 'then he'll get them as soon as he comes back. They might contain something important. Goodbye.'

When I got outside I stopped and said aloud in the middle of the street, clenching my fists, 'I will tell you one thing, my dear Lord – you are a so-and-so!' Then I nod furiously up at the clouds, gritting my teeth, 'I'll be damned, but you are a real so-and-so!'

I took a few steps and stopped again. Suddenly changing my posture, I fold my hands, lean my head sideways and ask in a sweet, sanctimonious voice, 'Have you indeed turned to him, my child?'

It didn't sound right.

'With a capital H, I say, with an H as big as a cathedral! Once more, "Have you indeed called upon Him, my child?"' Then I lower my head, make my voice sorrowful and answer, 'No.'

That didn't sound right either.

'You don't know how to act the hypocrite, you fool! Yes, you should say, yes, I have called upon my God and Father! And you should utter your words to the most pitiful tune you have ever heard. So, once more! Yes, that's better. But you have to sigh, sigh like a colicky horse. That's it.'

I walk along instructing myself like this, stamping my feet impatiently when I don't get it right and reviling myself for a blockhead, while the astonished passers-by turn around to watch me.

I chewed steadily on my wood shaving and shambled through the streets as fast as I could. Before I knew it, I was way down at Jærnbanetorvet Square. The clock of Our Saviour's showed half past one. I stopped a while, pondering. My face broke out in a faint sweat, it oozed its way down into my eyes. 'Come let's go for a walk to the pier!' I said to myself. 'That is, if you can spare the time.' And I bowed to myself and went down to Jærnbane Pier.

Out there were the ships, and the sea swayed in the sunshine. There was a hustle and bustle everywhere – blasting steam whistles, porters with crates on their shoulders, and lively sea shanties coming from the barges. Not far away from me sits a cake vendor, bending her brown nose over her merchandise; the small table in front of her is hideously loaded with dainties, and I turn away in distaste. She fills the entire quay with her kitchen odours; ugh, open the windows! I turn to a gentleman sitting next to me and try earnestly to make him see the nuisance of having cake vendors here, there and everywhere. . . . No? But surely he had to admit that . . . The good man smelled a rat, however, and didn't even let me finish what I had to say before getting up and leaving. I got up too and followed him, firmly set on convincing the man that he was wrong.

'For sanitary reasons, if for nothing else,' I said, patting him on the shoulder.

'Excuse me, I'm a stranger here and know nothing about the sanitary conditions,' he said, giving me a frightened stare.

Well, that altered the case, his being a stranger. . . .
Could I do him some favour? Show him around? No?
For it would be a pleasure to me, and it would cost him
nothing. . . .

But the man was dead set on getting rid of me and
rapidly crossed the street to the other pavement.

I went back to my bench again and sat down. I was
very restless, and the big barrel organ that had begun to
play a little further on made me even more so. A regular
metallic music, a snatch of Weber to which a little girl
sings a mournful ballad. The poignant flute-like sound of
the organ ripples through my blood, my nerves begin to
vibrate as though resonating with it, and a moment later I
fall back upon the bench, murmuring and humming along
with the music. What whims one's feelings give rise to
when one is starving! I feel caught up in these notes,
dissolved into a tune – I float, and I perceive so clearly
how I float, soaring high above the mountains, dancing
through realms of light. . . .

'A penny!' says the little organ-girl, holding out her tin
plate, 'just a penny!'

'Of course,' I answer automatically, jumping up and
rummaging through my pockets. But the child thinks I
just want to make fun of her and goes away immediately,
without a word. This mute resignation was too much for
me, it would have suited me better if she had scolded
me. Overcome with pain, I called her back. 'I don't have
a penny,' I said, 'but I'll remember you later, perhaps
tomorrow. What's your name?' That was a pretty name,
I wouldn't forget it. 'Till tomorrow, then . . .'

But I understood quite well that she didn't believe me,

although she never said a word, and I wept with despair that this little guttersnipe refused to believe me. I called her back once more, tore open my coat and wanted to give her my waistcoat. 'I'll make it all up to you,' I said, 'just wait a moment . . .'

I didn't have a waistcoat.

How could I even look for it! Weeks had gone by since it was in my possession. What was the matter with me anyway? Flabbergasted, the girl didn't wait any longer but beat a hasty retreat. And I had to let her go. People crowded together around me, laughing aloud. A police officer forces his way up to me and wants to know what's up.

'Nothing,' I answer, 'nothing at all. I just wanted to give my waistcoat to that little girl over there . . . for her father. . . . It's nothing to laugh at. I will simply go home and put on another one.'

'No rumpus in the street!' says the officer. 'So, move along now!' And he nudges me on my way. 'Are these your papers?' he shouts after me.

'Damn it, yes, my newspaper article, many important writings! How could I be so careless!'

I grab my manuscript, make certain that it is in the proper order, and leave without staying another moment or taking a look around, up at the editor's office. It was now four by the clock of Our Saviour's.

The office is closed. I steal noiselessly down the stairs, scared as a thief, and stop in a daze outside the gate. What should I do now? I lean up against the wall, staring down at the stone pavement and pondering. A pin lies gleaming before my feet, and I bend down and pick it up. What if

I removed my coat buttons, how much would I get for them? Maybe it wouldn't do me any good; buttons were just buttons. But I went ahead and examined them from all sides and found them to be as good as new. So it was a happy thought all the same, I could cut them loose with my half-penknife and take them over to the cellar. The hope of being able to sell these five buttons revived me instantly, and I said, 'It's going to be all right, you'll see!' My joy got out of control, and I began at once to remove the buttons, one after another. While doing so, I carried on the following silent chat with myself:

Well, you see, one has become rather poor – a momentary difficulty. . . . Worn-out, you say? Mind your tongue, please! I would like to see the person who wears out fewer buttons than I do. Let me tell you, I always go with my coat open; it has come to be a habit with me, an idiosyncrasy. . . . Oh well, if you don't *want* to. But I won't take less than ten øre for them, at a minimum. . . . No, good Lord, who ever said that you *have to* do it? You can just shut up and let me be. . . . All right, go ahead and *call* the police then. I'll wait here while you go and get the officer. And I won't steal anything from you. . . . Well, goodbye, goodbye! My name incidentally is Tangen, I've been out a bit late . . .

Then someone is on the stairs. I am instantly called back to reality, recognise Scissors, and hastily slip the buttons into my pocket. He wants to get by, doesn't even answer my greeting, is suddenly very busy inspecting his fingernails. I stop him and ask about the editor.

'He's not in.'

'You're lying!' I said. And with a nerve which made

me wonder at myself, I continued, 'I must talk to him, it's urgent. I have something to report from the Prime Minister's.'

'Why can't you tell it to me?'

'To you?' I said, giving Scissors the once-over.

It helped. He came straight back upstairs with me and opened the door. My heart was in my mouth. I clenched my teeth hard to bolster my courage, knocked and stepped into the editor's private office.

'Oh, hello! It's you,' he said cordially. 'Sit down.'

If he had shown me the door on the spot, it would have been more welcome. I was ready to cry and said, 'I beg your pardon—'

'Sit down,' he repeated.

So I sat down and explained that I had another article it was important for me to get into his paper. I had taken such pains with it, it had cost me much effort.

'I'll read it,' he said, taking it. 'Everything you write probably costs you some effort; but you are much too highly strung. If you could just be a little more level-headed! There's always too much fever. However, I'll read it.' And he turned back to his desk again.

There I sat. Did I dare ask him for a krone? Explain to him why there was always so much fever? Then he would be sure to help me; it wasn't the first time.

I got up. Hmm! But the last time I saw him he had complained about money, had even sent the bill collector out to scrape together some for me. Maybe it would be the same thing now. No, it mustn't happen. Couldn't I see that he was working?

'Is there anything else?' he asked.

'No,' I said, making my voice firm. 'When may I drop in again?'

'Oh, any time you pass by,' he answered. 'In a couple of days or so.'

I couldn't make my request pass my lips. This man's friendliness seemed to be boundless, and I would know how to appreciate it. Sooner starve to death. And I left.

Not even when I stood outside and could again feel the onslaught of hunger did I regret having left the office without asking for that krone. I took the other wood shaving out of my pocket and put it in my mouth. Again it helped. Why hadn't I done so before? 'You should be ashamed of yourself!' I said aloud. 'Could you really dream of asking this man for a krone and once again cause him embarrassment?' And I gave myself a proper tongue-lashing for this piece of impudence I had dreamed up. 'By God, that's the rudest thing I've ever heard!' I said – 'rushing at a man and nearly scratching his eyes out just because you need a krone, miserable dog that you are! So, move on! Faster! Faster, you lout! I'll teach you!'

I started running to punish myself, left street after street behind me at full blast, pushed myself on with suppressed shouts, and screamed mutely and furiously at myself whenever I felt like stopping. Meanwhile I had got to way up in Pilestrædet Lane. When I stood still at last, on the verge of tears from anger at not being able to run any further, my whole body trembled and I threw myself down on some steps. 'No, hold it,' I said. And to torture myself properly I got up again and forced myself to remain standing, and I laughed at myself and gloated over my own exhaustion. Finally, after several minutes had elapsed, I nodded, giving myself permission to sit down; but even then I chose the most uncomfortable spot on the steps.

God, how delicious it was to rest! I wiped the perspiration from my face and drank in the air in long, fresh gulps. How I had run! But I didn't regret it, I had it coming. Why had I wanted to ask for that krone anyway? Now I could see the consequences! And I began to talk gently to myself, giving the sort of admonitions a mother would. I grew more and more maudlin and, weak and tired, started crying. A quiet and heartfelt crying, an inward sobbing without a tear.

I sat on the same spot for a quarter of an hour or more. People came and went and nobody bothered me. Some children were playing here and there around me, and a little bird warbled in a tree on the other side of the street.

A policeman came up to me and said, 'Why are you sitting here?'

'Why am I sitting here?' I said. 'Because I like to.'

'I've been watching you for the last half hour,' he said. 'You've been sitting here for half an hour, haven't you?'

'Just about,' I answered. 'Anything else?' I got up angrily and left.

On reaching the marketplace I stopped and looked down at the ground. Because I like to! What sort of answer was that? Because I'm tired, you should have said, and you should have said it with a mournful voice – you're a blockhead, you'll never learn to act the hypocrite! – because of exhaustion! And you should have sighed like a horse.

When I got to the fire station I stopped again, stirred by a new idea. I snapped my fingers, burst into a loud laugh that astonished the passers-by and said, You know, now you should go and visit Levion, the parson. Yes, by golly, you really should. Well, just to try. What have you got to lose? Besides, it's such beautiful weather.

I entered Pascha's Bookshop, found the address of Pastor Levion in the city directory and started out. Now or never! I said. And don't try any tricks! Conscience, you say? No nonsense now; you're too poor to afford a conscience. You're hungry, don't forget, you've come on a matter of importance, the one thing most needful. But you must lay your head on your shoulder and make your voice tuneful. You don't want to? Then I won't go another step with you, now you know. Look, you are sorely troubled, fighting an awesome battle with the powers of darkness and with big, silent monsters at night, and you hunger and thirst for wine and milk and receive them not. That's the pass to which you've come. And here you are without as much as spit in your lamp. But you do believe in grace, thank God for that, you haven't yet lost your faith! And then you shall fold your hands and affect the believer in grace like the very devil. As far as Mammon is concerned, you hate Mammon in all his guises. As for a hymn book, that's a different matter, a remembrance worth a few kroner. . . . I stopped at the parson's door and read: 'Office hours from 12 to 4.'

No nonsense now! I said again, we're going through with it. So, down with your head, a little more. . . . I rang the bell at the private entrance.

'I'm looking for the pastor,' I said to the maid. I wasn't able, however, to include any mention of God.

'He's gone out,' she replied.

Gone out! Gone out! That ruined my plan, made a total muddle of everything I had meant to say. What had I gained, then, by this long walk? There I was.

'Is it something special?' the maid asked.

'Not at all!' I answered, 'not at all. We were just having such lovely God's weather that I felt like walking out here to pass the time of day.'

There I stood, and there she stood. I stuck out my chest on purpose to make her aware of the pin holding my coat together. I begged her with my eyes to see what I had come for, but the poor dear didn't understand a thing.

Such lovely God's weather, indeed. Wasn't the mistress home either?

Oh yes, but she had rheumatism and lay on a sofa unable to move. . . . Perhaps I would like to leave a message or something?

No, not at all. I just took walks like this every now and then, to get some exercise. It was so beneficial after dinner.

I started going back. What was the point of chatting any longer? Besides I had begun to feel dizzy; no mistake, I was about to crack up in real earnest. Office hours from 12 to 4; I had knocked an hour too late: the hour of grace was past.

At Stortorvet Square I sat down on one of the benches near the church. God, how black everything was beginning to look for me now! I didn't cry, I was too tired; utterly exhausted, I sat there without doing a thing, sat still and starved. My chest was most affected, smarting awfully with a curiously burning sensation. Nor would chewing wood shavings help anymore; my jaws were tired of their fruitless labour and I let them rest. I gave up. On top of it all, a piece of brown orange peel I had found in the gutter and immediately started gnawing at had made me nauseous. I was sick; the swollen veins in my wrists looked blue.

Why, then, had I been procrastinating? Running around the livelong day for the sake of a krone to keep body and soul together for a few more hours! When all was said and done, wasn't it a matter of indifference whether the inevitable happened one day earlier or one day later? If I had acted like a respectable person, I would have gone home and laid myself to rest a long time ago – given up. At this moment my mind was lucid: I was going to die. It was autumn now and everything had gone to sleep. I had tried every way out, made the most of every resource I knew of. I indulged myself sentimentally with this thought, and every time I still cherished hopes of a possible rescue I whispered dismissively, 'You fool, you've started to die already!' I ought to write a few letters, have everything ready, get prepared. I would wash myself with great care and fix up my bed nicely; I would lay my head on a few sheets of white writing paper, the cleanest thing I had left, and the green blanket I could . . .

The green blanket! The same instant I was wide awake, the blood rose to my head and my heart went pit-a-pat. I get up from the bench and start walking; with life stirring afresh in every recess of my body, I repeat over and over again these isolated words: The green blanket! The green blanket! I walk faster and faster, as though I had to catch up with something, and shortly I find myself at home in my tinsmith's shop once more.

Without pausing a moment or wavering in my decision, I go over to the bed and roll up Hans Pauli's blanket. I would be very surprised if this clever idea of mine didn't save me. I rose infinitely above the stupid misgivings that sprang up in me, I didn't give a hoot for them. I was no saint, carrying virtue to the point of idiocy, my sanity was intact. . . .

I took the blanket under my arm and went to 5 Stener Street.

I knocked and stepped into the large unfamiliar hall for the first time; the bell on the door gave lots of desperate strokes above my head. Chewing, his mouth full of food, a man comes in from an adjoining room and takes his place behind the counter.

'Please, lend me half a krone on my glasses!' I said. 'I'll redeem them in a couple of days, without fail.'

'What? They are steel frames, aren't they?'

'Yes.'

'No, I can't.'

'Well, no, I suppose you can't. Anyway, it was just idle talk. But here I've got a blanket that I really haven't any use for any more, and it occurred to me you might be willing to take it off my hands.'

'Unfortunately I have an entire storeroom full of bed-clothes,' he replied. And when I had unfolded it, he just threw one glance at it and shouted, 'Pardon me, but no, I haven't any use for it either.'

'I wanted to show you the poorest side first,' I said. 'The other side is much better.'

'Maybe so, but it's no use – I don't want it, and you won't get ten øre for it anywhere.'

'I know it isn't worth anything,' I said, 'but I thought it could be thrown in with another old blanket at the auction.'

'No, it won't do.'

'Twenty-five øre?' I said.

'No! I just don't want it, man, I won't have it in my house.'

I took the blanket under my arm again and went home.

I pretended to myself that nothing had happened, spread the blanket on the bed again, smoothed it nicely the way I used to, and tried to erase every trace of my last action. I couldn't possibly have had all my wits about me the moment I decided to play this dirty trick. The more I thought about it, the more preposterous it appeared to me. It must have been an attack of weakness, some relaxation in my innermost being that had caught me off guard. Anyway, I hadn't fallen into the trap, something told me I was letting myself in for trouble, and I had expressly tried with the glasses first. And I was extremely happy that I hadn't had the opportunity to go through with this sin, which would have stained the last hours of my life.

I wandered out onto the streets again.

I sat down once more on a bench near the Church of Our Saviour and dozed with my head on my breast, limp after my last excitement, sick and worn out with hunger. Time passed.

I had better sit out this hour, too; it was a bit lighter outdoors than in the house. Moreover, it seemed to me that my chest didn't labour quite so hard in the open air. I would get home soon enough anyway.

So I dozed and mused and suffered quite badly. I had picked up a little stone, which I brushed off and stuck in my mouth to have something to munch on. Otherwise I didn't stir, didn't even move my eyes. People came and went. The clatter of carriages, clopping of horses' hoofs, and talk filled the air.

I could try with the buttons though, couldn't I? But it obviously wouldn't do any good, and besides I was rather sick. On second thoughts, however, walking home I would have to go in the direction of 'Uncle's' – my proper 'Uncle's' – anyway.

I got up at last and dragged myself, slowly and shakily, along the streets. I began to feel a burning sensation above my eyebrows; a fever was coming on and I hurried along as best I could. Once more I passed the bakery with the loaf of bread in the window. Come, we won't stop here, I said with affected firmness. But what if I walked in and asked for a piece of bread? It was a fleeting thought, a flash. For shame! I whispered, shaking my head. And I walked on, bristling with irony at my own expense. I knew very well it was no use making any appeals for help in that shop.

In the Ropewalk, a pair of lovers were whispering in an entranceway; a little further on a girl stuck her head out of the window. I was walking so slowly and warily, I might have all sorts of ideas in my head – and the girl came out on the street.

'How are you, old man? What, are you sick? God help us, what a face!' And the girl beat a hasty retreat.

I stopped immediately. What was the matter with my face? Had I really started dying? I passed my hand up along my cheeks: thin – of course I was thin, my cheeks were like two bowls with the bottoms in. Oh Lord! I shuffled on.

But I stopped again. I must be just incredibly thin. My eyes were sinking deep into my skull. What, exactly, did I look like? The devil only knew why you had to be turned into a veritable freak just because of hunger! I experienced rage once more, its final flare-up, a spasm. God help us, what a face, eh? Here I was, with a head on my shoulders without its equal in the whole country, and with a pair of fists, by golly, that could grind the town porter to fine dust, and yet I was turning into a freak from hunger, right here in the city of Kristiania! Was there any rhyme or reason in that? I had put my shoulder to the wheel and toiled day and night, like a nag lugging a parson; I had read till my eyes were bursting from their sockets and starved till my wits took leave of my brain – and where the hell had it gotten me? Even the streetwalkers prayed to God to free them from the sight of me. But now it was going to stop, understand; it was going to *stop*, or I'd be damned! . . . With ever-increasing rage, grinding my teeth in response to my fatigue, sobbing and cursing, I continued to rant and rave, paying no heed to the people passing by. I began once more to torture myself, running my head against the lampposts on purpose, digging my fingernails deep into the backs of my hands, and biting my tongue in frenzy when it didn't speak clearly, and I laughed madly whenever it fairly hurt.

'Yes, but what shall I do?' I asked myself at last. I stamp my feet on the pavement several times and repeat, 'What shall I do?' A gentleman just walking by remarks with a smile, 'You should go and ask to be locked up.'

I looked after him. It was one of our well-known women's physicians, going by the name 'the Duke'. Not even he understood my condition, a man I knew and whose hand I had shaken. I fell silent. Locked up? Of course, I was mad; he was right. I felt the insanity in my blood, felt it tearing through my brain. That was what I would come to, was it? Oh, well. I resumed my slow, sad walk. So that was where I would end up!

All of a sudden I stop again. But not locked up, I say, not that! I was almost hoarse with fear. I begged for mercy, making wild entreaties not to be locked up. For then I would land in jail again, be confined in a dark cell where there wasn't a glimmer of light. Not that! There were other ways open which I hadn't yet tried. I would try them; I would work harder at it, take my time, walk tirelessly from house to house. There was Cisler, the music dealer, for example, I hadn't been to him at all. Something would be sure to turn up. . . . I went along talking this way until I made myself cry from emotion once more. Anything rather than being locked up!

Cisler? Was this perhaps a higher hint, a pointer? His name had occurred to me for no reason at all and he lived so far away, but I would go and see him all the same, walking slowly and resting every now and then. I knew the place, had been there often in the good old days to buy sheet music. Should I ask him for a half-krone? That might embarrass him; I had better ask for a whole krone.

I entered the store and asked for the boss; I was shown into his office. There he sat, a handsome and fashionably dressed man, looking through some papers.

I stammered forth an apology and stated my errand. Forced by need to turn to him. . . . Wouldn't be too long before I should pay him back. . . . As soon as I received the fee for my newspaper article. . . . He would be doing me such a kindness. . . .

Even while I was talking he turned back to his desk and went on with his work. When I was through he gave me a sidelong glance, shook his handsome head and said, 'No.' Simply no. No explanation. Not a word.

My knees shook violently and I leaned against the small polished counter. I had to try once more. Why should exactly his name occur to me as I was standing way down in the Vaterland section? I felt repeated twitches in my left side and I started perspiring. Hmm. I was really terribly run-down, I said, quite sick, I was afraid. It would almost certainly be no more than two or three days before I could pay him back. If he would be so kind?

'My dear man, why do you come to me?' he said. 'You are a perfect stranger to me, come in straight off the street. Go to the paper, where they know you.'

'Only for tonight,' I said. 'The office is closed now and I'm very hungry.'

He kept shaking his head, continued to shake it even after I had my hand on the latch.

'Goodbye,' I said.

There wasn't any higher hint or pointer, I thought,

smiling bitterly; as high as that I could point, too, if it came to that. I struggled along street after street, resting briefly on some front steps every once in a while. If only I didn't get locked up! My dread of the cell pursued me all along, refusing to leave me alone; every time I saw a policeman ahead of me, I shuffled into a side street to avoid meeting him. Now we'll count one hundred steps, I said, and try our luck again! Something will turn up eventually.

It was a small yarn shop, a place where I had never set foot before. A lone man behind the counter, an office further back with a porcelain name plate on the door, long rows of packed shelves and tables. I waited until the last customer had left the shop, a young lady with dimples. How happy she looked! I decided against trying to impress her with the pin in my coat and turned away.

'Can I help you?' the assistant asked.

'Is the boss in?' I said.

'He's on a hiking tour in the Jotunheimen mountains,' he replied. 'Is it something special?'

'It's about a few øre for a meal,' I said, trying to smile. 'I'm hungry and I haven't got a single øre.'

'Then you're just as rich as I am,' he said, and set about arranging some parcels of yarn.

'Oh, don't turn me away – not now!' I said, suddenly feeling cold all over. 'Believe me, I'm almost dead with hunger, it's been many days since I had anything to eat.'

With the utmost seriousness, without saying a word, he started turning his pockets inside out, one by one. Wouldn't I take his word for it?

'Just five øre,' I said. 'And I'll give you ten back in a couple of days.'

'My dear man, do you want me to steal from the till?' he asked impatiently.

'Yes,' I said. 'Yes, take five øre from the till.'

'I don't do that sort of thing,' he wound up. Then he added, 'And while we're at it, let me tell you I've had enough of this.'

I dragged myself out, sick with hunger and hot with shame. Really, this would have to stop! Things had gone too far with me. I had held my head above water for so many years, I'd kept upright in such hard times, and now all of a sudden I had lowered myself to the crassest sort of panhandling. This one day had brutalised my mind through and through, spattered my heart with shamelessness. I'd had the gall to become maudlin, shedding tears in front of petty shopkeepers. And what good had it done me? Wasn't I still without a piece of bread to stick in my mouth? I had managed to make me disgusted with myself. Yes, it had to stop, right now! But at this very moment they were locking the gate at home, and I had to hurry if I didn't want to spend the night in the jail again.

This gave me strength, I didn't want to spend the night in jail. My body bent over, one hand pressed against my left ribs to ease the stinging pain a little, I struggled on, keeping my eyes fixed upon the pavement to avoid forcing eventual acquaintances to say hello, and hurried over to the fire station. Thank God, it was only seven by Our Saviour's clock, I had still three hours before the gate closed. How scared I had been!

I had now done everything I could, no stone had been

left unturned. That a whole day should go by without my succeeding even once! I thought. If I told that to someone, nobody would believe me, and if I wrote it down they would say it had been fabricated. Not in a single place! Well, it couldn't be helped; above all, don't go around being maudlin anymore. Ugh, how sickening – on my word, it makes me feel disgusted with you! When all hope was gone, it was gone. By the way, couldn't I steal a handful of oats in the stable? A shaft of light, a stray beam – I knew that the stable was locked.

I took it easy, crawling homeward at a snail's pace. I felt thirsty, happily for the first time all day, and kept looking around for a place to drink. I had got too far away from the Arcades, and I didn't want to walk into a private house. Perhaps I could just wait till I got home, it would take a mere quarter of an hour. It was by no means certain that I could keep down a mouthful of water anyway; my stomach didn't tolerate anything any more, I even felt nauseated by the saliva I kept swallowing.

But the buttons! I hadn't tried with the buttons yet. I stood stock-still and broke into a smile. There might still be a way out. I wasn't completely doomed. I would certainly get ten øre for them, tomorrow I would get ten more someplace or other, and Thursday I would be paid for my newspaper article! There you could see, things would take a turn for the better! Imagine forgetting the buttons! I took them out of my pocket and inspected them as I walked on; my eyes went dim with joy, and I couldn't properly see the street I was walking on.

How thoroughly familiar I was with that big cellar, my refuge in the dark evenings, my bloodsucking friend!

One by one my possessions had vanished down there, little things from home, my last book. I would go down to watch on the auction day, and I was glad every time my books seemed to fall into good hands. Magelsen, the actor, had my watch, and that made me almost feel proud; a yearbook with my first modest poetic attempts in it had been bought by an acquaintance, and my overcoat ended up with a photographer, to be on loan in the studio. So I had no reason to complain.

I held the buttons ready in my hand and stepped in. 'Uncle' sits at his desk, writing.

'I'm not in a hurry,' I say, afraid to disturb him and rub him up the wrong way with my request. My voice sounded so strangely hollow that I almost failed to recognise it, and my heart was thumping like a hammer.

He approached me with a smile as usual, placed both his hands palms down on the counter, and looked me squarely in the face without saying anything.

Well, I had brought something I wanted to ask if he could use . . . something that was only in my way at home – 'Believe me, a real nuisance, some buttons.'

Well, what about it, what about those buttons? And he brings his eyes right down to my hand.

Couldn't he let me have a few øre for them? . . . As much as he himself saw fit. . . . Using his own discretion. . . .

'For those buttons?' 'Uncle' stares at me in surprise. 'For *these* buttons?'

Just enough for a cigar or whatever he pleased to give me. 'I was just passing by and thought I'd drop in.'

The old pawnbroker laughed and returned to his desk

without saying a word. I just stood there. I hadn't really hoped for very much, and yet I had thought I might possibly be helped out. This laughter was my death sentence. It probably wasn't any use to try with the glasses either.

'Naturally I would throw in my glasses, too, that goes without saying,' I said, taking them off. 'Just ten øre' – or, if he pleased, five øre.

'You know, don't you, that I can't lend you anything on your glasses,' 'Uncle' said. 'I have told you so before.'

'But I need a stamp,' I said, in a muffled voice. I couldn't even mail the letters I was going to write. 'A ten- or five-øre stamp, just as you please.'

'May God bless you, and now, be on your way!' he answered, motioning me off with his hand.

All right, we'll forget about it, I said to myself. Mechanically, I put my glasses back on, picked up the buttons and left. I said good night and closed the door behind me as usual. There, nothing more to be done! I stopped at the top of the stairs and took another look at the buttons. Imagine, he wasn't at all interested! I said. And the buttons are almost new; I just can't understand.

While I stood there, absorbed in these reflections, a man came by and went down into the cellar. In his hurry he had brushed against me, we both apologised, and I turned around and followed him with my eyes.

'Oh, it's you!' he suddenly said, from the bottom of the stairs. He came back up and I recognised him. 'Goodness gracious, you look a mess!' he said. 'What were you doing down here?'

'Oh – I had some business. You're going there too, I see.'

'Yes. What did you bring?'

My knees shook, I leaned against the wall and held out my hand with the buttons.

'What the hell!' he cried. 'No, this is going too far!'

'Goodnight,' I said, turning to go. I had a lump in my throat.

'No, wait a moment!' he said.

What should I wait for? He was on his way to 'Uncle' himself, bringing his engagement ring perhaps, had been going hungry for several days, was in debt to his land-lady.

'All right,' I answered, 'if you will be quick—'

'Of course,' he said, grabbing my arm. 'But the fact is, I don't believe you, idiot that you are. You'd better come with me.'

I understood what he had in mind, felt another twinge of honour all of a sudden and answered, 'I can't! I've promised to be in Bernt Anker Street at half past seven, and—'

'Half past seven, yes! But it's eight now. See this watch in my hand? That's what I'm taking down there. So, in with you, you hungry sinner! I'll get at least five kroner for you.'

And he pushed me in.

Part Three

A week went by in joy and gladness.

I was over the worst this time too. I had food every day, my courage rose, and I had more and more irons in the fire. I was working on three or four monographs, which picked my poor brain clean of every spark, every thought that arose in it, and I felt it was going better than before. My last article, which had cost me so much running around and given rise to so much hope, had already been returned by the editor, and I had destroyed it immediately, angry and insulted, without reading it afresh. In the future I would try another paper, in order to open up more opportunities for myself. At worst, if that didn't help either, I had the ships to turn to. *The Nun* lay ready to sail at the pier, and I might be able to work my way to Arkhangelsk on it, or wherever it was bound for. So there was no lack of prospects in several quarters.

My last crisis had dealt roughly with me. I began to lose a lot of hair, my headaches were also very troublesome, especially in the morning, and my nervousness refused to go away. During the day I sat and wrote with my hands swathed in rags, merely because I couldn't stand my own breath on them. When Jens Olai slammed the stable door downstairs or a dog entered the back yard and started barking, I felt as though pierced to the marrow by cold stabs of pain which hit me everywhere. I was fairly done for.

I toiled at my work day after day, barely allowing myself time to gulp down my food before going on with my writing again. In those days both my bed and my small wobbly writing table were flooded with notes and manuscript pages I took turns working on, adding new things that would occur to me in the course of the day, erasing, brushing up the dead spots with a colourful word here and there, struggling ahead sentence by sentence with the greatest difficulty. Then, one afternoon, one of my articles was finished at last and, pleased and happy, I stuck it in my pocket and went up to the 'Commander'. It was high time I bestirred myself to get some money again, I didn't have very many øre left.

The 'Commander' asked me to sit down for a moment, then he would right away. . . . And he went on writing.

I looked about me in the small office: busts, lithographs, clippings, and an immense wastebasket that looked as though it could swallow a man whole. I felt sad at the sight of this huge maw, these dragon's jaws which were always open, always ready to receive fresh scrapped writings – fresh blasted hopes.

'What is today's date?' the 'Commander' suddenly asks from his desk.

'The 28th,' I answer, glad to be of service to him.

'The 28th.' And he goes on writing. Finally he slips a

couple of letters into their envelopes, tosses some papers into the wastebasket, and lays down his pen. Then he swings around in his chair and looks at me. When he notices that I am still standing by the door, he waves his hand in a half-serious, half-facetious manner and points to a chair.

I turn away so he won't see I'm not wearing a vest when I open my coat, and take the manuscript from my pocket.

'It's just a short profile of Correggio,' I say, 'but I'm afraid it may not be written in such a way that—'

He takes the papers out of my hand and starts leafing through them. He turns his face in my direction.

So this was how he looked close up, this man whose name I had already heard in my first youth and whose paper had had the greatest influence on me throughout the years. His hair is curly, his fine brown eyes a bit restless; he has a habit of snorting slightly every once in a while. A Scottish parson couldn't look more gentle than this dangerous writer, whose words had always left bloody stripes wherever they struck. I am stirred by a curious feeling of fear and admiration vis-à-vis this person; on the verge of tears, I cannot help advancing a step to tell him how sincerely I loved him for all he had taught me and to ask him not to hurt me – I was only a poor devil who had a hard enough time of it as it was.

He looked up and slowly folded my manuscript, pondering as he did so. To make it easier for him to give me a refusal, I extend my hand slightly and remark, 'Oh well, you can't use it, of course.' And I smile to give the impression I'm taking it lightly.

'Everything we can use must be so popular,' he answers. 'You know the sort of public we have. Couldn't you try to make it a bit simpler? Or else come up with something that people understand better?'

His tact strikes me with wonder. I realise that my article has been scrapped, but I couldn't have received a nicer refusal. So as not to take up more of his time, I reply, 'Yes, I suppose I could.'

I walk up to the door. Hmm. He had to excuse me for taking up his time with this. . . . I bow and put my hand on the doorknob.

'If you need it,' he says, 'I would be glad to give you a small advance. You can always write for it.'

Now that he had seen I was no good as a writer, his offer felt somewhat humiliating, and I replied, 'Thank you, no, I can manage a while yet. Thank you kindly anyway. Goodbye.'

'Goodbye,' the 'Commander' replies, turning back to his desk the same moment.

Even so he had treated me with undeserved kindness, and I was grateful to him for that; I would know how to appreciate it, too. I decided not to come back to him until I could bring him a piece I was completely satisfied with, something that would take the 'Commander' by surprise and make him order me to be paid ten kroner without a moment's hesitation. I returned home and set about writing afresh.

The next several evenings, as eight o'clock approached and the street lamps had already been lighted, the following happened regularly to me:

As I come out of my entranceway in order to set out on

a walk in the streets after the day's labour and hardships, a lady dressed in black stands near the lamppost just outside the gate. Her face is turned toward me, and she follows me with her eyes as I walk past her. I notice that she is always dressed the same way, wears the same heavy veil that conceals her face and falls over her breast, and carries in her hand a small umbrella with an ivory ring in the handle.

It was already the third evening I had seen her there, always in the very same spot. As soon as I had passed, she turned slowly and walked down the street, away from me.

My nervous brain shot out its feelers, and I immediately had the absurd idea that her visit concerned me. In the end I was nearly on the point of accosting her, asking her if she was looking for someone, if she needed my help with something, or if I could take her home – poorly dressed though I was, regretfully – and protect her in the dark streets. But I had a vague fear it might cost me something, a glass of wine or a cab ride, and I didn't have any money left. My hopelessly empty pockets had an all too disheartening effect on me, and I didn't even have the courage to look closely at her as I walked past. Hunger had again begun to play havoc with me, I hadn't had a bite to eat since last night. That certainly wasn't a very long time, I had often been able to hold out for several days on end, but I had begun to grow alarmingly thinner. I wasn't nearly as good at starving as I used to be; a single day could now put me into a near daze, and I suffered from constant vomiting as soon as I drank some water. Moreover, I was cold at night – sleeping in my clothes, the same I'd worn all day, I was blue with cold, chilled to the bone and shivering every night, and I froze stiff in my sleep. The old blanket couldn't keep out the draft, and I woke up in the morning with a stuffed nose because of the sharp, hoar-frosty air that penetrated my room from outside.

I wander about the streets trying to figure out how to keep my head above water until I finish my next article. If only I had a candle. Then I could try to slog away into the night, a couple of hours was all it would take once I got into my stride. And tomorrow I could call on the 'Commander' again.

Without further ado, I enter the Oplandske Café to look for my young acquaintance from the bank and touch him for ten øre to buy a candle. They let me pass from room to room unchallenged; I passed a dozen tables where chatting customers sat eating and drinking, pressed all the way to the back of the café, into the Red Room, without finding my man. Embarrassed and annoyed, I crawled out into the street again and started walking in the direction of the Palace.

Why the hell, why the living everlasting hell, wouldn't my tribulations ever end! Taking long furious strides, my coat collar turned raffishly up in the back and my hands clenched in my trouser pockets, I cursed my unlucky stars every step of the way. Not a truly carefree moment in seven to eight months, not the bare necessities of life for an entire short week before want once again brought me to my knees. And on top of it all, here I had gone around being honest in the midst of my misery, hee-hee, fundamentally honest anyway! Good heavens, what a fool

I had been. And I began to tell myself how I had even gone around with a bad conscience because I had once taken Hans Pauli's blanket to the pawnbroker. I laughed scornfully at my tender scruples, spat contemptuously in the gutter and was at a loss for words that were strong enough to deride myself for my folly. It should have been now! Were I to find on the street, this minute, a schoolgirl's modest savings, a poor widow's last penny, I would snatch it up and stick it in my pocket, steal it in cold blood and sleep like a log all night afterwards. I hadn't suffered so unspeakably for nothing, my patience was up, I was ready for anything.

I walked around the Palace three or four times and then decided to go home, took yet another turn into the park and finally went back down Karl Johan Street.

It was around eleven. The street was rather dark and people were strolling about everywhere, a jumble of quiet couples and noisy groups. The great moment had arrived, the mating hour when the secret traffic takes place and the jolly adventures begin. Rustling skirts, a few bursts of sensual laughter, heaving breasts, excited, panting breaths; far down, by the Grand Hotel, a voice calling, 'Emma!' The entire street was a swamp, with hot vapours rising from it.

I instinctively search my pockets for two kroner. The passion quivering in every movement of the passers-by, the dim light of the street lamps, the tranquil, pregnant night – it was all beginning to affect me: this air filled with whispers, embraces, trembling confessions, half-spoken words, little squeals. Some cats are making love amid loud shrieks in Blomquist's entranceway. And I didn't have two kroner. It was a torment, a misery like no other, to be so impoverished. What humiliation, what disgrace! And again I came to think of the poor widow's last mite which I would have stolen, the schoolboy's visored cap or hanky, the beggar's haversack which I would have taken to the rag dealer without any fuss and wasted on drink. To take comfort and make it up to myself, I began to see all sorts of faults in these happy people who were gliding by; I shrugged my shoulders angrily and looked disdainfully at them as they passed by, couple after couple. These easily satisfied, sweet-munching students who thought they were cutting loose in Continental style if they could feel a seamstress's bosom! These young gentry, bank clerks, merchants, boulevard dandies who didn't even turn up their noses at sailors' wives, fat duckies from the cattle market who would flop down in the nearest doorway for a crock of beer! What sirens! The place beside them still warm from last night's fireman or groom, the throne always equally vacant, equally wide open – please, step right up! . . . I gave a long spit over the sidewalk, without bothering whether it might hit someone, angry with and full of contempt for these people who were rubbing up against one another and pairing off before my very eyes. I lifted my head and felt deep down how blessed I was to be able to follow the straight and narrow.

At Storting Place I met a girl who looked hard at me as I came alongside.

'Good evening,' I said.

'Good evening.' She stopped.

'Hmm.' She was out for a stroll so late? Wasn't it a

bit risky for a young lady to walk on Karl Johan Street at this time of night? No? But wasn't she ever accosted or molested – 'I mean, to put it bluntly, asked to come home with someone?'

She looked at me in surprise, examining my face to see what I could mean by this. Then she suddenly slipped her hand under my arm and said, 'Come along.'

I went with her. When we were a few steps past the cab rank, I stopped, freed my arm and said, 'Listen, my friend, I don't have a penny.' And I prepared to go.

At first she refused to believe me, but when she had gone through all my pockets without anything turning up, she got peeved, tossed her head and called me a dry stick.

'Goodnight,' I said.

'Wait a minute,' she called. 'Those are gold-rimmed glasses, aren't they?'

'No.'

'Then go to hell!'

And I went.

Shortly afterward she came running after me and called me once more. 'You can come anyway,' she said.

I felt humiliated by this offer from a poor streetwalker and said no. Besides, it was getting late and I had to be somewhere; nor could she afford such sacrifices.

'No, now I *want* you to come.'

'But I won't go with you under those circumstances.'

'You're on your way to someone else, of course,' she said.

'No,' I answered.

Alas, I had no real bounce in me these days. Women had become almost like men to me. Want had dried me up. But I felt I was cutting a sorry figure vis-à-vis this strange tart and decided to save face.

'What's your name?' I asked. 'Marie? Well, listen, Marie.' And I started explaining my behaviour. The girl became more and more astonished. So she had thought that I, too, was one of those types who walked the streets at night chasing little girls? Did she really think that badly of me? Had I by any chance said anything rude to her up to now? Did men behave the way I did if they had something wicked in hand? In short, I had accosted her and walked those few steps with her to see how far she would go. My name, by the way, was such and such, Pastor this or that. 'Goodnight! Go, and sin no more!'

With that I left.

I rubbed my hands in delight at my clever idea and talked aloud to myself. What a joy it was to go around doing good deeds! I might have given this fallen creature a nudge towards redemption for the rest of her life! She would appreciate it when she managed to collect herself; what's more, she would remember me in her dying hour, her heart full of gratitude. Ah, how rewarding it was to be honest and upright! My spirits were absolutely radiant, I felt as fit as could be and game for anything. If only I had a candle, then perhaps I could finish my article. I was dangling my new key in my hand as I walked along, humming, whistling, and pondering a way to procure a candle. I had no choice but to take my writing materials downstairs, out on the street, under the lamp. I opened the gate and went up to get my papers.

When I came back down I locked the door from the outside and stationed myself under the light from the lamp.

It was quiet all around; I could hear only the heavy, clanking footfalls of a policeman in the side street and, far away, in the direction of St Hanshaugen, a dog barking. There was nothing to disturb me, I pulled my coat collar up around my ears and started thinking with all my might. It would be a wonderful help to me if I were lucky enough to come up with the conclusion to this little monograph. I was at a rather difficult point right now, to be followed by a quite imperceptible transition to something new, and then a muted, gliding finale, a long-drawn-out rumble which would finally end in a climax as bold, as shocking, as a shot or the sound of a cracking rock. Full stop.

But the words wouldn't come. I read through the entire piece from the beginning, read each sentence aloud, but I just couldn't collect my thoughts for this crashing climax. On top of everything, as I stood there trying to work it out, the policeman came up and planted himself in the middle of the street a little way off, spoiling my entire mood. What business was it of his if at this moment I was working on an excellent climax to an article for the 'Commander'! Good God, how absolutely impossible it was for me to keep my head above water, no matter how hard I tried! I stood there for about an hour. The policeman went away. It was getting too cold to be standing still. Crestfallen and discouraged by another wasted effort, I finally opened the gate and went up to my room.

It was very cold up there, and I could barely see my window in the thick darkness. I groped my way over to the bed, pulled off my shoes and set about warming my feet between my hands. Then I lay down – just as

I was, fully clothed, as I had been doing now for a long time.

The following morning I sat up in bed as soon as it was light and set to work on my article once more. I sat there like that until noon, by which time I had managed to write ten or twenty lines. And I still hadn't reached the finale.

I got up, put on my shoes and started pacing the floor to warm up. The windowpanes were coated with ice; I looked out – it was snowing, and down in the back yard the pavement and the pump were covered by a thick blanket of snow.

I puttered about in my room, took listless turns back and forth, scratched the walls with my fingernails, leaned my forehead carefully against the door, tapped the floor with my forefinger and listened attentively – all without an object, but done quietly and thoughtfully as though I were engaged on a matter of some importance. And all the while I said aloud, time after time, so I could hear it myself, 'But good Lord, this is mad!' Still, I carried on as insanely as ever. After a long time, perhaps a couple of hours, I pulled myself sharply together, bit my lip and braced up as best I could. This had to end! I found a sliver to chew on and promptly set about writing again.

A few brief sentences got done with great effort, a dozen or two miserable words that I forced out at all costs simply to make some progress. Then I stopped – my head was empty and I didn't have the strength to go on. When I just couldn't get any further, I began staring with wide-open eyes at those last words, that unfinished sheet of paper, peering at the strange, trembling letters which stared up at me from the paper like small unkempt figures, and at the end I understood nothing at all and didn't have a thought in my head.

Time passed. I could hear the traffic in the street, the noise from carriages and horses. Jens Olai's voice floated up to me from the stable when he talked to the horses. I was completely listless, moistening my lips a little every once in a while but otherwise doing nothing. My chest was in a sorry state.

It began to get dark. I drooped more and more, grew tired and lay back on the bed. To warm my hands a bit, I passed my fingers through my hair, back and forth and criss-cross; small tufts of hair trailed along, loosened wisps that stuck to my fingers and spread over the pillow. I didn't stop to think about it right then, it didn't seem to concern me, and besides I had plenty of hair left. I tried once more to shake off this strange drowsiness, sliding like a fog through all my limbs; I sat up, beat my knees with the palms of my hands and coughed as hard as my chest would allow, only to fall back again. Nothing helped; I was fading helplessly away with open eyes, staring straight at the ceiling. Finally I stuck my forefinger in my mouth and took to sucking on it. Something began stirring in my brain, some thought in there scrabbling to get out, a stark-staring mad idea: what if I gave a bite? And without a moment's hesitation I squeezed my eyes shut and clenched my teeth together.

I jumped up. I was finally awake. A little blood trickled from my finger, and I licked it off as it came. It didn't hurt, the wound was nothing really, but I was at once brought back to my senses. I shook my head, went over to the window and found a rag for the wound. While I was fiddling with this, my eyes filled with water – I wept softly to myself. The skinny lacerated finger looked so sad. God in heaven, to what extremity I had come!

The darkness grew more impenetrable. If only I had a candle, then I could possibly write the finale in the course of the evening. My head was clear once more. Thoughts came and went as usual and I didn't suffer particularly; I didn't even feel my hunger as badly as a few hours ago, I could surely hold out till the following day. Maybe I could get a candle on credit if I went to the grocer's and explained my situation. I knew the place so well; in the good old days, when I could still afford it, I had bought many a loaf of bread in that shop. There wasn't the slightest doubt that they would let me have a candle on the strength of my good name. For the first time in a long while I brushed my clothes a bit and removed the loose hairs on my coat collar, as far as the darkness allowed. Then I groped my way down the stairs.

When I got out on the street, it occurred to me that perhaps I ought to ask for a loaf of bread instead. I grew doubtful and stopped to think. No way! I finally answered myself. I was unfortunately not in a condition to tolerate food right now; it would be the same story all over again, with visions and intimations and crazy ideas, and my article would never get finished. I had to show up at the 'Commander's' before he forgot me again. No way! I decided on a candle. And so I entered the shop.

A woman stands at the counter making purchases; several small parcels, wrapped in different kinds of paper, are lying beside me. The assistant, who knows me and knows what I usually buy, leaves the woman, wraps a loaf of bread in a newspaper straightaway, and puts it in front of me.

'No – actually it is a candle this evening,' I say. I say it very softly and humbly so as not to irritate him and spoil my chances of getting the candle.

My answer came as a surprise to him, it was the first time I had asked for something other than bread from him.

'Then you'll have to wait a moment,' he says, turning back to the woman.

She gets her things and pays, handing him a five-krone bill on which she receives change, then leaves.

The assistant and I are now alone.

He says, 'And then there was your candle.' He tears open a pack of candles and takes one out for me.

He looks at me and I look at him, I cannot bring myself to voice my request.

'Oh, that's right, you paid already,' he says suddenly. He says simply that I had paid, I heard every word. And he begins to count out silver coins from the till, one krone after another, fat shiny coins – he gives me back change on five kroner, the woman's five-krone bill.

'There you are!' he says.

I stare at these coins for a second, feeling that something is wrong; I don't reflect, my mind is a blank, I'm just stunned by all this wealth that lies gleaming before my eyes. I gather up the money automatically.

I stand there outside the counter, dumbfounded, vanquished, annihilated; I take a step toward the door and stop again. I direct my gaze at a certain point on the wall; a little bell in a leather collar hangs there and,

125

beneath it, a bundle of string. I stand staring at these articles.

The assistant, who thinks I would like to strike up a chat, seeing that I'm taking my time, says as he tidies up some wrapping paper floating around on the counter, 'It looks like we're going to have winter now.'

'Hmm. Yes,' I answer, 'it looks like we're going to have winter now. It does look like it.' A moment later I add, 'Well, it's none too early. But it does, indeed, look like it. It's certainly none too early, for that matter.'

I could hear myself uttering this drivel, but took in each word I spoke as though it were coming from another person.

'Do you really think so?' the assistant says.

I put the hand with the money in my pocket, grabbed the latch and left; I could hear myself saying goodnight and the assistant answering.

When I had gone a few steps away from the stairs, the shop door was flung open and the assistant called after me. I turned around without surprise, without a trace of fear; I just gathered the coins in my hand and prepared to give them back.

'Here you are, you forgot your candle,' the assistant says.

'Ah, thank you,' I answer calmly. 'Thanks! Thanks!'

And I walked on down the street, carrying the candle in my hand.

My first rational thought concerned the money. I went over to a street lamp and counted it afresh, weighing the coins in my hand and smiling. So, in spite of everything, here I was magnificently helped out – impressively and wonderfully helped out for a long, long time! And I stuck my hand, with the money, back in my pocket and went off.

I stopped outside a cellar eatery on Storgaten Way, considering coolly and calmly whether I should venture to take a light lunch right away. I could hear the clatter of plates and knives inside and the sound of meat being beaten. The temptation was too great, I went in.

'A beefsteak!' I say.

'A beefsteak!' the waitress called through a service hatch.

I settled down by myself at a small table just inside the door and began to wait. It was somewhat dark where I sat, I felt fairly well hidden and started thinking. Every now and then the waitress glanced over at me with a certain curiosity.

My first real dishonesty had been committed, my first theft, compared to which all my previous shenanigans counted for nothing; my first tiny, big fall. . . . Very well! There was nothing to be done about that. Anyway, it was all up to me, I would straighten it out with the shopkeeper afterwards, later on, when it was more convenient. I didn't have to go any further down that path; at the same time, I hadn't undertaken to live any more honestly than other people, there was no agreement. . . .

'Will the steak be coming soon, do you think?'

'Yes, quite soon.' The waitress opens the service hatch and looks into the kitchen.

But what if the matter came to light? What if the assistant were to get suspicious, begin to ponder the episode with the loaf of bread, the five-krone bill the woman got change for? It was by no means impossible that he would some day catch on, perhaps the next time I went there. Oh, dear me! . . . I shrugged my shoulders on the sly.

'Here you are!' the waitress says kindly, putting the steak on the table. 'But wouldn't you rather move to another room? It's so dark in here.'

'No, thanks, just let me stay here,' I answer. Her friendliness touches me all of a sudden, and I pay for the steak right away, giving her whatever coins I get hold of in my pocket and closing her hand over them. She smiles, and I say in jest, with moist eyes, 'Keep the rest to buy yourself a farm. . . . Oh, you're welcome!'

I began to eat, grew more and more ravenous every minute and gobbled up big chunks without chewing them. I tore at the meat like a cannibal.

The waitress came over to me again.

'Wouldn't you like to have something to drink?' she says. And she bends down slightly toward me.

I looked at her; she spoke in a very low voice, almost shyly. She lowered her eyes.

'I mean a pint of beer or whatever you'd like . . . on me . . . no charge. . . . If you'd like to . . .'

'No, thank you very much!' I answered. 'Not now. I'll come back some other time.'

She withdrew and sat down behind the counter; I could only see her head. A strange person!

When I was finished I walked straight to the door. I felt sick already. The waitress got up. I was afraid to enter the lighted area, fearing to expose myself too much to this young girl who had no idea of my misery, so I said a quick goodnight, bowed and left.

The food began to take effect, it gave me great pain and I wasn't allowed to keep it for very long. I emptied my mouth in every dark corner I passed, struggling to suppress the nausea that was hollowing me out afresh, clenching my fists to make myself tough, stamping my feet on the pavement and furiously gulping down again whatever wanted to come up – but in vain! I ran at last into an entranceway where, hunched over and blinded with the water that flooded my eyes, I emptied myself once again.

Overcome by wrath, I walked down the street sobbing, cursing the cruel powers, whoever they might be, that were persecuting me so, blasting them with eternal damnation and everlasting torment for their meanness. These powers showed little chivalry, mighty little chivalry indeed, take it from me! . . . I went over to a man who was staring through a shop window and asked him in all haste what, in his opinion, one should offer a person who had gone hungry for a long time. It was a matter of life and death, I said; he couldn't stand beef.

'I've heard that milk is supposed to be good, boiled milk,' the man answers, utterly astonished. 'Who are you asking for anyway?'

'Thanks! Thanks!' I say. 'Yes, that may be quite good, boiled milk.'

And I go my way.

At the first café I came across I went in and asked for some boiled milk. I got the milk, gulped it down hot as it was, swallowed every drop greedily and left again. I headed for home.

Then something strange happened. Outside my gate,

leaning against the lamppost and flush in the light from the lamp, stands a person whom I can make out dimly already a long way off – it's the lady dressed in black again. That same lady in black as on the previous evenings. There was no mistaking it, she had shown up on the very same spot for the fourth time. She stands perfectly motionless.

I find this to be so odd that I instinctively slacken my steps. At this moment my thoughts are in proper order, but I am all worked up, my nerves being irritated by my last meal. I walk straight past her as usual, get almost to the door and am about to step inside. Then I stop. I have a sudden inspiration. Without trying to understand why, I turn around, walk straight up to the lady, look her full in the face and say, 'Good evening, miss.'

'Good evening,' she answers.

Excuse me, but was she looking for somebody? I had noticed her before, could I help her in any way? 'My sincere apologies, by the way.'

Well, she wasn't quite sure . . .

Nobody lived along this entranceway except for three or four horses and me, it happened to be a stable and a tinsmith's shop. I was afraid she was on the wrong track altogether if she kept looking for somebody here.

She turns her face away and says, 'I'm not looking for anyone, I'm just standing here.'

Really, she was just standing there, standing there like that night after night just because of a whim. That was a bit odd; the more I thought about it, the more puzzled I became by the lady. Then I decided to be bold. I jingled the coins in my pocket and invited her straight off to have a glass of wine with me someplace or other . . . to celebrate the coming of winter, hee-hee. . . . It didn't have to take very long. . . . But maybe she'd rather not?

No thanks, she thought she'd better not. No, she couldn't do it. But if I would be so kind as to walk with her part of the way, then. . . . It was quite dark going home, and she felt uncomfortable walking up Karl Johan Street alone at such a late hour.

'With pleasure.'

We started off; she walked on my right-hand side. A peculiar, lovely feeling took hold of me. The consciousness of being in the presence of a young girl. I didn't take my eyes off her throughout our walk. The perfume in her hair, the warmth radiating from her body, this fragrance of woman that surrounded her, that sweet breath every time she turned her face towards me – all this streamed in upon me, penetrating irresistibly all my senses. I could just barely make out a full, somewhat pale face behind her veil and a high bosom that strained against her coat. The thought of all this hidden loveliness, whose presence I sensed under her coat and behind her veil, was bewildering to me and made me idiotically happy without any sensible reason. I couldn't hold back any longer and touched her with my hand, fingering her shoulder and smiling daftly. I could hear my heart pounding.

'How strange you are!' I said.

'Really? In what way?'

Well, for one thing she was plainly in the habit of standing motionless in front of a stable door night after night for no purpose whatsoever, just because it came into her head. . . .

Oh, but she might have her reasons for doing that.

Besides, she loved staying up late at night, she had always liked that a lot. Was I myself keen on going to bed before twelve?

I? If there was one thing in the world I hated, it was going to bed before twelve at night. 'Ha-ha!'

'Ha-ha, there you see!' And so she would take a walk like this in the evening when she had nothing better to do. She lived up on St Olaf Place—

'Ylajali!' I cried.

'What was that?'

'I only said Ylajali. . . . All right, go on!'

She lived up on St Olaf Place, a rather lonesome spot, with her mama, who it was no use talking to because she was so hard of hearing. So was it to be wondered at that she liked to spend some time out of the house?

'No, not at all,' I answered.

'Well, what then?' I could tell by her voice that she was smiling.

Didn't she have a sister?

Yes, an elder sister – how did I happen to know that? But she had gone to Hamburg.

'Recently?'

'Yes, five weeks ago.' Who had told him that she had a sister?

Nobody had, I just asked.

There was a silence. A man walks past with a pair of shoes under his arm, otherwise the street is empty as far as the eye can see. Over by the amusement park is a long shining row of coloured lamps. The snow had stopped. The sky was clear.

'Good heavens, aren't you cold without an overcoat?' the lady says suddenly, looking at me.

Should I tell her why I wasn't wearing an overcoat? Let her know my situation right away and frighten her off, now just as well as later? How delightful it was, though, to walk here at her side and keep her in the dark a little while longer. I lied and answered, 'No, not at all.' And to change the topic, I asked, 'Have you seen the menagerie in the amusement park?'

'No,' she answered. 'Is it worth seeing?'

What if she took it into her head she wanted to go there? Into all that light, among so many people! It would be far too embarrassing for her, I would scare her away with my shabby clothes and my emaciated face, which I hadn't washed for two days. She might even discover I didn't have a waistcoat. . . .

So I answered, 'Well, no, I suppose it's not worth seeing.' Then some happy thoughts occurred to me which I made use of right away, a few cheap words, leavings from my dried-up brain: What, after all, could one expect from such a small menagerie? In general, I wasn't interested in seeing animals in cages. These animals know that you are watching them; they feel those hundreds of curious eyes and are affected by them. No, let us have animals that don't know you are watching them, those shy creatures puttering about in their winter lairs, lying there with somnolent eyes, licking their paws and thinking. Eh?

Yes, I was certainly right about that.

It was the animal with all its peculiar awesomeness and peculiar wildness there was something special about. Those stealthy, noiseless steps in the dead of night, the

soughing and eeriness of the forest, the screeching of a
bird flying past, the wind, the smell of blood, the rumble
from space – in short, the spirit of the wild in the wild
beast. . . .

But I was afraid that this bored her, and the feeling
of my extreme poverty beset me anew and weighed me
down. If only I had been reasonably well-dressed, then
I could have made her happy with that walk in the
amusement park. I couldn't understand this person who
was able to take pleasure in letting herself be escorted up
the whole length of Karl Johan Street by a half-naked
tramp. What in God's name was she thinking of? And
why was I putting on an act like this, smiling at nothing
like an idiot? What sensible reason did I have for letting
myself be dragged along on such a long walk by this
dainty bird of paradise? Wasn't it, in fact, taxing my
strength? Didn't I feel the chill of death go straight to
my heart at even the gentlest puff of wind that blew
our way? And wasn't madness already clamouring in my
brain from mere lack of food for many months on end?
She even prevented me from going home and sipping a
bit of milk, another spoonful of milk I could maybe keep
down. Why didn't she just turn her back on me and let
me go to blazes . . .?

I grew desperate; my hopelessness drove me to extremes
and I said, 'You shouldn't really be walking here with me,
miss; I compromise you in the eyes of everybody by my
clothes alone. Yes, it's quite true, I mean it.'

She's taken aback. She looks quickly up at me, without
a word. Then she says, 'Good heavens!' Nothing more.

'What do you mean by that?' I asked.

'Oh dear, don't say such things. . . . We haven't got very far to go now.' And she walked a little faster.

We turned the corner at University Street and could see the lights on St Olaf Place already. Then she walked more slowly again.

'I hate to be indiscreet,' I remark, 'but won't you tell me your name before we part? And won't you lift your veil for just one moment so I can see you? I would be so grateful.'

Pause. I was waiting.

'You've seen me before,' she answers.

'Ylajali!' I say again.

'You followed me once for half a day, all the way home. Were you drunk that time?' I could hear again that she was smiling.

'Yes,' I said. 'Yes, I'm afraid I was drunk that time.'

'That was mean of you!'

Contrite, I admitted it was mean of me.

Then we were at the fountain – we stop and look up at the many illuminated windows of number 2.

'This is as far as you can walk with me,' she says. 'Thanks for taking me home.'

I bowed, not daring to say a word. I doffed my hat and stood bareheaded. I wondered if she would give me her hand.

'Why don't you ask me to walk back with you part of the way?' she says playfully. But she looks down at the tip of her shoe.

'Oh,' I answer, 'if you only would!'

'All right, but only a little way.'

And we turned around.

I was utterly bewildered, I didn't know which way was up any more; this person turned all my thinking topsy-turvy. I was enchanted, wonderfully glad; I felt as though I were dying from happiness. She had expressly wanted to go back with me, it wasn't my idea, it was her own wish. I gaze and gaze at her, growing more and more cocky, and she encourages me, drawing me toward her by every word she speaks. I forget for a moment my poverty, my humble self, my whole miserable existence, I feel the blood coursing warmly through my body as in the old days, before I broke down. I decided to feel my way with a little trick.

'By the way, it wasn't you I was following that time,' I said. 'It was your sister.'

'Was it my sister?' she says, greatly astonished. She stops and looks at me, positively expecting an answer. She was asking in deadly earnest.

'Yes,' I answered. 'Hmm. That is, it was the younger of the two ladies who were walking ahead of me.'

'The younger? Aha!' She laughed, at once loud and sincerely, like a child. 'Oh, how sly you are! You said that just to get me to lift my veil. I understood that much. But you won't get your way . . . for punishment.'

We began to laugh and joke, talking incessantly all the time; I didn't know what I was saying, I was happy. She told me she had seen me once before, a long time ago, in the theatre. I was with three friends and I had behaved like a madman; I must have been drunk that time too, she was afraid.

Why did she think so?

Oh, I had laughed so much.

'Really. Yes, I used to laugh a lot in those days.'

'But not any more?'

'Oh of course, now too.' It was glorious just to be alive!

We were approaching Karl Johan Street. She said, 'Now we won't go any further.' We turned around and walked back up University Street. When we reached the fountain again, I slowed down a bit, knowing I had walked her as far as I could go.

'So, now you'll have to turn around,' she said, stopping.

'Yes, I suppose I must,' I answered.

But a moment later she thought I could certainly walk her to the door. Good heavens, there was nothing wrong with that, was there?

'No,' I said.

But as we stood there by the door, all my misery again bore down upon me. Anyway, how could you keep up your courage when you were so broken-down? Here I stood before a young woman, dirty, tattered, disfigured by hunger, unwashed, only half-dressed – it was enough to make you sink into the ground. I made myself small and ducked instinctively as I said, 'You won't meet me again, will you?'

I had no hope that she would let me see her again; I was almost wishing for a sharp no, which would brace me up and make me indifferent.

'Oh, yes,' she said.

'When?'

'I don't know.'

Pause.

'Won't you, please, lift your veil for just a moment?' I said, 'so I can see who I've been talking with? One moment, that's all. Because, you know, I must see who I've been talking with.'

Pause.

'You can meet me Tuesday evening, right here,' she says. 'Would you like to?'

'Dear, yes, if you'll let me!'

'Eight o'clock.'

'Good.'

I passed my hand down over her coat, brushing away the snow to have a pretext for touching her. It gave me a thrill to be so close to her.

'And try not to think badly of me, will you?' she said. She smiled again.

'No—'

Suddenly she made a resolute movement and pulled her veil up over her forehead. We stood looking at each other for a second. 'Ylajali!' I said. She rose on her toes, flung her arms around my neck and kissed me right on the lips. I could feel her bosom heaving, hear her rapid breath.

She broke away from me at once, called good night in a whisper, breathlessly, turned around and ran up the stairs without another word.

The front door slammed shut.

The following day it snowed harder, a heavy snow mixed with rain, big blue flakes that fell on the ground and turned to mud. The air was raw and freezing cold.

I had woken up rather late, my head strangely confused

by the emotions of the previous evening, my heart intoxicated from that beautiful encounter. In my rapture I had
lain awake a while imagining Ylajali beside me; I spread
my arms, hugged myself and blew kisses in the air. Then I
had finally turned out, got myself another cup of milk and
soon afterward a steak, and I wasn't hungry any more.
Only, my nerves were greatly agitated again.

I went down to the clothing stalls. It occurred to me
that I might pick up a second-hand waistcoat at a bargain
price, something to wear under my coat, no matter what.
I walked up the steps to the stall and found a waistcoat
that I began to examine. While I was busying myself with
this an acquaintance came by; he nodded and called to
me, and I let the waistcoat hang and went down to him.
He was a technician, on his way to the office.

'Come and have a glass of beer with me,' he said. 'But
hurry up, I don't have much time. . . . Who was that
woman you were walking with last night?'

'Look here, you!' I said, jealous of his mere thought.
'What if she was my sweetheart?'

'I'll be damned!' he said.

'Oh yes, it was all decided yesterday.'

I had bowled him over, he believed me unquestioningly.
I stuffed him full of lies to get rid of him. We got our beer,
drank up and left.

'Goodbye, then! . . . Look,' he said suddenly, 'I owe you
a few kroner, you know, and it's a shame I haven't paid
you back a long time ago. But you'll get your money by
and by.'

'All right, thanks,' I replied. But I knew he would never
pay me back that money.

The beer went to my head right away unfortunately, and I felt very hot. The thought of last night's adventure overwhelmed me, made me almost distraught. What if she didn't show up on Tuesday! What if she began to mull it over and get suspicious! . . . Suspicious about what? . . . My thoughts, suddenly alive and kicking, started grappling with the money. I felt deadly afraid, appalled at myself. The theft rushed in upon me in every particular: I saw the little shop, the counter, my skinny hand as I grabbed the money, and I pictured to myself how the police would proceed when they came to pick me up. Shackles on hands and feet, no, only on the hands, maybe only on one hand; the desk, the register of the officer on duty, the sound of his scratchy pen, his glance, his dangerous glance: Ah, Mr Tangen? The cell, the eternal darkness. . . .

Hmm. I clenched my fists hard to bolster my courage, walked more rapidly and came to Stortorvet Square. Here I sat down.

No kid's stuff now! How in the world could they prove that I had stolen anything? Besides, the grocery boy wouldn't dare sound the alarm, even if he should remember how it had all happened some day; his job was too dear to his heart for that. No commotion, no scenes, if you please!

But the coins still felt heavy in my pocket and gave me no peace of mind. I set about testing myself and discovered as clear as could be that I had been happier before, when I was suffering in all honesty. And Ylajali! Hadn't I also dragged her down with my sinful hands? Oh Lord, oh Lord my God! Ylajali!

Feeling drunk as a coot, I suddenly jumped up and went right over to the cake vendor near the Elephant Pharmacy. I could still recover from my disgrace, it was far from too late, I would show the whole world that I had it in me to do so! On the way I got the money ready, holding every øre in my hand. I bent forward over the woman's table as if I wanted to buy something and smacked the money into her hand, just like that. I didn't say a word and left at once.

How wonderful to be an honest person again! My empty pockets no longer felt heavy, it was a pleasure to be broke once more. All things considered, I had to admit that this money had cost me much secret anguish, I had thought of it with a veritable shudder time and again. I was no hardened soul, my honest nature had revolted from the base deed, oh yes. Thank God, I had raised myself in my own estimation! I defy you to do as much! I said, looking out over the crowded marketplace, just you try! I had made a poor old cake vendor ever so happy, she didn't know which way to turn. Her children wouldn't go to bed hungry tonight. . . . I worked myself up with these thoughts, feeling that I had acted splendidly. Thank God, the money was now out of my hands.

Drunk and nervous, I walked down the street, girding up my loins. My delight at being able to meet Ylajali pure and honest and to look her squarely in the face, quite ran away with me in my drunkenness. I felt no pain any more and my head was clear and empty; it was as if I had a head of pure shining light on my shoulders. I had a mind to do mischief, commit some startling act, turn the town topsy-turvy and raise a rumpus. All the way up Grænsen

Street I behaved like a madman; there was a faint ringing in my ears, and in my brain the intoxication was going full tilt. Carried away by rashness, I took it into my head to go and report my age to a town porter, who incidentally hadn't said a word, grab his hand, fix him with a penetrating look, and leave him again without an explanation. I could distinguish the nuances in the voices and the laughter of the passers-by, observed some small birds hopping ahead of me in the street, began to study the expressions of the cobblestones and discovered all sorts of signs and quaint figures in them. Meanwhile I had reached Storting Place.

I suddenly stand still, staring down at the cabs. The coachmen wander about talking among themselves, the horses hang their heads against the foul weather. Come! I said, nudging myself with my elbow. I walked quickly up to the first carriage and climbed in. '37 Ullevaal Road!' I cried. And we rolled off.

En route the coachman started to look behind him, leaning down and peeping into the carriage, where I was sitting under the oilskin. Had he become suspicious? There was no doubt that my miserable get-up had caught his eye.

'I have to see a certain man,' I called out, to steal a march on him, and I earnestly explained that I absolutely had to see this man.

We stop outside number 37. I jump out, run up the stairs, all the way to the third floor, grab a bell rope and give it a tug. The bell gave six or seven dreadful jangles inside. .

A girl opens the door. I notice that she's wearing gold

earrings, and has black lasting-buttons on her grey bodice.
She looks at me in dismay.

I ask for Kierulf, Joachim Kierulf, if she would oblige,
a trader in wool – in short, there was no mistaking
him. . . .

The girl shakes her head. 'There's no Kierulf living
here,' she says.

She stares at me and takes hold of the door, ready
to beat a retreat. She made no effort to find the man;
she really looked like she knew the person I was asking
for, if she would just stop and think, the lazy creature.
I got angry, turned my back on her and ran down the
stairs again.

'He wasn't there!' I called to the coachman.

'Wasn't he there?'

'No. Drive to 11 Tomte Street.'

I was in a most violent frenzy, which rubbed off on the
coachman too – he evidently believed it was a matter of
life and death and drove off without further question. He
lashed his horse on.

'What is the man's name?' he asked, turning around
on the cox.

'Kierulf, the wool trader, Kierulf.'

The coachman also seemed to think there was no
mistaking that man. Didn't he usually wear a light-
coloured coat?

'What's that?' I cried. 'A light coat? Are you mad? Do
you imagine I'm asking for a cup of tea?' This light coat
was extremely unwelcome and spoiled the image of the
man I had made for myself.

'What did you say his name was? Kierulf?'

'Certainly,' I answered. 'Is there anything strange about that? What's in a name anyway?'

'Doesn't he have red hair?'

It might very well be that he had red hair, and now that the coachman mentioned it, I was instantly convinced he was right. I felt grateful to the poor driver and told him he had caught the spitting image of the man; what he had said was perfectly correct. It would be something quite exceptional, I said, to see such a man without red hair.

'It must be the same person I've driven a couple of times,' the coachman said. 'He even had an ashplant.'

This made the man come vividly alive to me, and I said, 'Ha-ha, to be sure, no one has ever yet seen that man without his ashplant in his hand. You may rest assured as far as that goes, quite assured.'

Yes, it was obviously the same man he had driven. He had recognised him. . . .

We tore along, making the horse's shoes throw off sparks.

In the midst of this agitated state I hadn't for a single moment lost my presence of mind. We pass a police officer, and I notice his number is 69. This figure hits me with a terrible accuracy, it sticks in my brain instantly, like a splinter. Sixty-nine, exactly 69, I would never forget it!

A prey to the wildest fancies, I leaned back in the carriage, curled up under the oilskin hood so that no one could see I was moving my lips, and took to chattering idiotically to myself. Madness rages through my brain and I let it rage, fully aware of being subject to influences I cannot control. I began to laugh, noiselessly and passionately, without a trace of a reason, still jolly and drunk from the couple of glasses of beer I had had. Gradually my agitation subsides, my calm returns more and more. Feeling a chill in my sore finger, I stuck it inside my neck band to warm it a bit. We arrived thus at Tomte Street. The coachman reins up.

I alight from the carriage without haste, absent-mindedly, limply, my head heavy. I walk in through the gate, come into a back yard, which I cross, run into a door which I open and pass through, and find myself in a hallway, a kind of anteroom with two windows. In one corner stand two trunks, one on top of the other, and against the long wall an old, unpainted sofa bed with a blanket on it. In the next room, to the right, I can hear voices and the squalling of babies and, above me, on the second floor, the sound of someone hammering on an iron slab. I notice all this as soon as I enter.

I walk quietly straight across the room, over to the opposite door, without hurrying, without any thought of flight, open it too and step out into Vognmand Street. I glance up at the house I have just walked through and read above the door: 'Refreshments and Lodging for Travellers'.

It never enters my head to try and get away, giving the coachman waiting for me the slip. I walk sedately through Vognmand Street without fear and without being conscious of having done anything wrong. Kierulf, this trader in wool who had been haunting my brain for so long, this person who I thought existed and whom I perforce had to see, had vanished from my thoughts, erased together with other mad inventions that came and went by turns. I didn't remember him any more except as a vague feeling, a memory.

I sobered up more and more as I wandered on, feeling heavy and limp and dragging my feet. The snow was still falling in big, wet dollops. I got to the Grønland section at last, as far as the church, where I sat down on a bench to rest. All who walked past looked at me in great surprise. I became lost in thought.

Good God, what an awful state I was in! I was so thoroughly sick and tired of my whole wretched life that I didn't find it worth my while to go on fighting in order to hang onto it. The hardships had got the better of me, they had been too gross; I was so strangely ruined, nothing but a shadow of what I once was. My shoulders had slumped completely to one side, and I had fallen into the habit of leaning over sharply when I walked, in order to spare my chest what little I could. I had examined my body a few days ago, at noon up in my room, and I had stood there and cried over it the whole time. I had been wearing the same shirt for weeks on end, it was stiff with old sweat and had gnawed my navel to bits. A little blood and water was oozing from the wound, though it didn't hurt; but it was so sad to have this wound in the middle of one's stomach. I had no remedy for it, and it refused to heal by itself; I washed it, wiped it carefully and put on the same old shirt again. There was nothing to be done about it. . . .

I sit there on the bench mulling over all this and feeling quite dismal. I am disgusted with myself, even my hands appear loathsome to me. This flabby, shameless expression on the backs of my hands pains me, makes me uneasy. I feel rudely affected by the sight of my bony fingers, and I hate my whole slack body and shudder at having to carry it, to feel it around me. God, if only it would end! I yearned to die.

Completely defeated, defiled and degraded in my own estimation, I got up mechanically and began to walk homeward. On my way I passed a gate where one could read the following: 'Shrouds at Madam Andersen's, main entrance to the right'. Old memories! I said, remembering my previous room at Hammersborg, the little rocking chair, the newspaper wall-covering down by the door, the ad from the Director of Lighthouses and the freshly baked bread of Fabian Olsen, the baker. Well, yes, I had been much better off then than now; one night I had written a story worth ten kroner, now I couldn't write anything any more – I was completely unable to, my head grew empty as soon as I tried. Yes, I wanted to end it all! I walked and walked.

As I got closer and closer to the grocer's, I had a semiconscious feeling that I was approaching a danger; but I stuck to my purpose: I was going to give myself up. I walked calmly up the steps. In the doorway I meet a little girl carrying a cup in her hand, and I let her pass and close the door. The assistant and I stand face to face for the second time.

'Why,' he says, 'awful weather we're having.'

What was the point of this detour? Why didn't he just apprehend me at once? I became furious and said, 'I haven't come here to chat about the weather.'

My anger takes him aback, his little huckster's brain breaks down; it had never even crossed his mind that I had cheated him out of five kroner.

'You don't know that I have bamboozled you, do you?' I say impatiently, breathing heavily, trembling and ready to use force if he won't get to the matter in hand at once.

But the poor man is quite unsuspecting.

Good heavens, the sort of blockheads one had to live with! I shout at him, explaining to him point by point how it had all occurred, showing him where I stood and where he stood when the deed took place, where the coins had been, how I had gathered them up in my hand and closed my fingers over them – and he understands everything but still doesn't do anything about it. He turns this way and that, listens for footsteps in the next room, shushes me to get me to talk lower and finally says, 'That was a mean thing to do!'

'No, wait a minute!' I cried, feeling an urge to contradict him and egg him on. It wasn't as base or shabby as he, with his miserable grocer's mind, had imagined. I didn't keep the money, obviously, that would never occur to me; I didn't want to reap any benefit from it personally, that went against the grain of my thoroughly honest nature.

'So what did you do with it?'

I gave it away to a poor old woman, every penny, I wanted him to know. I was that kind of person, I never quite forgot the poor. . . .

He ponders this a while, evidently beginning to have doubts whether I am an honest man or not. Finally he says, 'Shouldn't you have returned the money instead?'

'No, just listen,' I answer brashly. 'I didn't want to get you into trouble, I wanted to spare you. But that's the thanks one gets for being magnanimous. Here I'm explaining the whole thing to you, which should make you cringe with shame, and yet you do nothing at all to settle the dispute between us. Therefore I'm washing my hands of it all. And besides, you can go to hell. Goodbye!'

I left, slamming the door behind me.

But when I got home to my room, into this miserable hole, soaked from the wet snow and my knees shaking from the day's wanderings, I lost my cockiness instantly and collapsed afresh. I regretted my attack on the poor shop assistant, wept, grabbed hold of my throat to punish myself for my dastardly trick and kicked up an awful row. He had naturally been deadly anxious about his job, hadn't dared make a fuss about the five kroner the business had lost. And I had exploited his fear, had tortured him with my loud talk, transfixing him with every word I yelled out. The boss himself had perhaps been sitting in the next room, within an ace of feeling called upon to come out and see what was going on. Why, there was no limit any more to the sort of vile things I was capable of.

All right. But why had I not been run in? Then it would be over with. After all, I had practically held out my hands for the irons. I wouldn't have put up the least resistance, rather I would have helped them. Lord of heaven and earth, one day of my life for a happy second once again! My whole life for a mess of pottage! Hear me just this once! . . .

I went to bed in my wet clothes. I had a vague idea that I might die during the night, and I used my last strength to fix up my bed a little so it would look fairly tidy around me in the morning. I folded my hands and chose my position.

All at once I remember Ylajali. That I could have forgotten her so completely all evening! A faint light penetrates my mind again, a tiny ray of sun, making me feel wonderfully warm. And the sunlight increases, a mild delicate silken light that brushes me in such a soothingly delicious way. The sun grows stronger and stronger, scorching my temples and seething white-hot and heavy in my emaciated brain. In the end a mad fire of sunbeams blazes before my eyes, a heaven and earth set on fire, humans and animals of fire, mountains of fire, devils of fire, an abyss, a desert, a whole world on fire, a raging Judgment Day.

And I saw and heard no more. . . .

The next morning I awoke in a sweat, damp all over; the fever had been quite rough on me. At first I had no clear awareness of what had happened to me; I looked about me in surprise, felt my nature had been totally changed, and could no longer recognise myself. I passed my hands up along my arms and down my legs, wondered at the window being where it was and not on the wall directly opposite, and heard the stomping of the horses down in the yard as if it came from above. I also felt rather nauseous.

My hair lay damp and cold around my forehead. I got up on my elbow and looked down at the pillow: wet hair there too, left behind in small tufts. My feet had swollen inside my shoes during the night, but they weren't painful, I just wasn't able to move my toes very much.

As the afternoon wore on and it was beginning to grow dark, I got out of bed and started pottering about the room. I felt my way with short, careful steps, making sure I kept my balance and sparing my feet as much as possible. I didn't feel much pain and I didn't cry; I wasn't at all sad, rather felt wonderfully contented. It didn't enter my mind just then that anything could be different than it was.

Then I went out.

The only thing that still bothered me a little was my hunger, despite the fact that food made me nauseous. I was beginning to feel an outrageous appetite again, a ravenous inner craving for food that was constantly growing worse and worse. There was a merciless gnawing in my chest, a queer silent labour was going on in there. I pictured a score of nice teeny-weeny animals that cocked their heads to one side and gnawed a bit, then cocked their heads to the other side and gnawed a bit, lay perfectly still for a moment, then began anew and bored their way in without a sound and without haste, leaving empty stretches behind them wherever they went.

I wasn't ill, just weak, and I broke into a sweat. I had meant to go over to Stortorvet Square to take a brief rest, but it was a long, difficult walk. Finally I was almost there, standing at the corner of the marketplace and Torv Street. The sweat trickled down into my eyes, fogging up my glasses and blinding me, and I had just stopped to wipe my face. I didn't notice where I was standing, gave it no thought. The noise around me was terrible.

Suddenly a shout rings out, a cold, sharp warning. I hear this shout, hear it very well, and jump nervously to one side, stepping as quickly as my poor legs would allow. A monster of a baker's van sweeps past me and the wheel grazes my coat; if I had been a bit quicker I would have gotten off scot-free. I could have been a bit quicker perhaps, a little bit quicker, if I had exerted myself. But there it was: one foot hurt, a couple of toes were crushed – I could feel how they sort of curled up inside my shoe.

The driver reins in his horses with all his might; he turns around in the van and asks, terrified, how it went. Oh, well, it could have been much worse . . . no big deal really . . . I didn't think any bones had been broken. . . . It's quite all right. . . .

I walked over to a bench as fast as I could; all those people who stopped to stare at me had made me feel embarrassed. It wasn't a deathblow after all, as far as accidents went it had turned out relatively well. The worst thing about it was that my shoe had been crushed to pieces, the sole torn loose at the tip. Lifting my foot, I could see blood in the gap. Oh well, it wasn't done willfully by either party, it hadn't been the man's intention to make things even worse than they were for me; he looked very frightened. If I had asked him for a small loaf of bread from his van, maybe I would have got it. He would probably have been glad to give it to me. May God give him joy in return, wherever he is!

I was terribly hungry and didn't know where to turn because of my shameless appetite. I twisted and turned on the bench and pressed my chest against my knees. When it got dark I trudged over to the jail – God knows how I got there – and sat down on the edge of the balustrade. I ripped a pocket out of my coat and started chewing on it, without any particular purpose, frowning angrily and staring into space with unseeing eyes. I heard some small children playing around me and sensed instinctively when a pedestrian went by. Otherwise I observed nothing.

Then I suddenly take it into my head to go down to one of the stalls in the arcade below me and lay hold of a piece of raw meat. I get up, cross the balustrade, step over to the far end of the arcade roof and walk down the stairs. When I was almost at the meat stand, I shouted up the empty stairway, shaking my fist as if talking to a dog up there, and turned brazenly to the first butcher I saw.

'Oh, please give me a bone for my dog!' I said. 'A bone, nothing more; there doesn't have to be anything on it. Just so he can have something to carry in his mouth.'

I got a bone, a gorgeous little bone with still a bit of meat left on it, and stuck it under my coat. I thanked the man so heartily that he looked at me in surprise.

'Forget it,' he said.

'Oh, don't say that,' I mumbled, 'it's very kind of you.'

I went back up. My heart was pounding.

I sneaked into the Smiths' Passage, as far back as I could get, and stopped in front of a tumbledown gate in a rear court. There wasn't a light to be seen anywhere, it was delightfully dark around me; I started gnawing my bone.

It had no taste at all; a sickening smell of dried blood rose from the bone and I had to vomit immediately. I tried again – if I could just keep it down, it would be sure to do some good, the important thing was to make it stay down. But I vomited again. I got angry, ground my teeth into the meat, ripped off a small piece and forced myself

153

to swallow it. It was no use: as soon as the tiny bits of meat grew warm in my stomach, up they came again. Frantic, I clenched my fists, burst into tears from helplessness and gnawed like mad; I cried so hard, the bone got wet and dirty from my tears – I threw up, cursed and gnawed again, crying as if my heart would break, then threw up once more. I swore at the top of my voice, damning all the powers of this world to eternal torment.

Quiet. Not a soul around, no light, no noise. I find myself in a most violent frenzy, breathing heavily and loudly and sobbing bitterly each time I have to give up these bits of meat which might alleviate my hunger. Since it avails me nothing however hard I try, I fling the bone at the gate, bursting with impotent hatred and carried away with rage, and shout fierce threats up at the heavens, screaming God's name hoarsely and savagely and crooking my fingers like claws . . . : 'I say to you, you holy Baal of heaven, you do not exist, but if you did exist I would curse you until your heaven trembled with the fires of hell. I say to you, I have offered you my service and you turned it down, you pushed me away, and now I turn my back on you for ever, because you did not know the time of your visitation. I say to you, I know I shall die and yet I mock you, Our Heavenly Apis, with death before my eyes. You have used force against me, and you do not know that I never bend in adversity. Ought you not to know that? Did you frame my heart in your sleep? I say to you, my whole body and every drop of blood in me rejoice in mocking you and spitting on your grace. From this moment on I shall renounce all your works and all your ways, I shall curse my thoughts if they ever think of you again and tear off my lips if they speak your name. I say to you, if you exist, the last word in life and in death, I say goodbye. And now I shall be silent, turn my back on you and go my way. . . .'

Quiet.

Quivering with rage and exhaustion, I keep on standing in the same place, still whispering oaths and insults, catching my breath after my fit of crying, broken and limp after my insane explosion of anger. Alas, it was nothing but rhetoric and literature, which I tried to get right even in the midst of my misery – it turned into a speech. I stood there maybe for half an hour, gasping and whispering while holding onto the gate. Then I hear voices, a conversation between two men who are coming toward me down the Smiths' Passage. I stagger away from the gate, drag myself along the walls of the buildings and come out onto the bright streets again. As I shuffle down Youngsbakken Lane, my brain suddenly begins to act in an extremely strange manner. It occurs to me that those wretched hovels at the edge of the marketplace, the storage shacks and the old stalls with second-hand clothing, were a real disgrace to the place. They spoiled the entire appearance of the marketplace and were a blot on the city – ugh, away with the junk! As I walked along, I turned over in my mind what it would cost to move the Geodetic Survey down there, that handsome building which had always appealed to me so much each time I passed it. It might not be possible to undertake a move of that kind for less than seventy to seventy-two thousand kroner – a tidy sum, one had to admit, quite a neat piece of change, hee-hee, to start with anyway. And I nodded my empty head and admitted that it was quite a nice bit of change to start with. My whole body was still shaking, and I gave deep gasps every now and then after my bout of tears.

I had a feeling there wasn't much life left in me, that I was in fact nearing my journey's end. It mattered very little to me one way or another, I didn't trouble my head about it in the least. Rather, I bent my steps downtown, towards the docks, further and further away from my room. For that matter, I could just as well have lain right down in the street to die. My sufferings were making me more and more insensitive: my sore foot was throbbing badly, indeed I had the impression that the pain was spreading up the entire leg, but even that didn't hurt very much. I had endured worse sensations.

I reached the Jærnbane Pier. There was no traffic, no noise, only a lone soul to be seen here and there, a stevedore or a sailor loafing about with his hands in his pockets. I noticed a lame man who squinted hard at me as we passed each other. I stopped him instinctively, touched my hat and asked if he knew whether *The Nun* had sailed yet. Afterward I couldn't help snapping my fingers right to his face and saying, 'Yes, damn it, *The Nun*!' *The Nun*, which I had completely forgotten! The thought of it must have slumbered unconsciously within me anyhow, I had borne it with me unknown to myself.

Lord, yes, *The Nun* had sailed.

He couldn't tell me where it had sailed to, could he?

The man thinks a moment, standing on his longer leg and holding the shorter one in the air; the shorter one swings a little.

'No,' he says. 'You wouldn't know what cargo it's been taking in?'

'No,' I reply.

But by now I had already forgotten *The Nun*, and I asked the man how far it might be to Holmestrand, in terms of good old geographic miles.

'To Holmestrand? I would guess—'

'Or to Veblungsnæs?'

'What I meant to say, I reckon that to Holmestrand—'

'Listen, come to think of it,' I interrupted him again, 'you wouldn't be so kind as to give me a quid of tobacco, would you, just a tiny little bit?'

I got the tobacco, thanked the man very warmly and walked off. I didn't make any use of the tobacco, I just stuck it in my pocket right away. The man was still keeping an eye on me, maybe I had somehow aroused his suspicion; standing or walking, I felt his suspicious glance following me, and I didn't like being persecuted by this individual. I turn around and drag myself over to him again, look at him and say, 'Welter.'

Only this one word: Welter. No more. I looked very hard at him as I said it, I felt I was glaring at him; it was as though I were looking at him from another world. I stood there for a moment after uttering this word. Then I shuffled up to Jærnbanetorvet Square again. The man didn't let out a sound, he just kept an eye on me.

Welter? All at once I stopped in my tracks. Sure. Wasn't it just what I had sensed from the very beginning: I had met this cripple before. Up in Grænsen Street one bright morning; I had pawned my waistcoat. It seemed like an eternity since that day.

As I am thinking about this – I'm leaning against a building at the corner of the marketplace and Havn Street – I give a sudden start and try to scramble off. Failing in this, I stare aghast straight ahead and swallow my shame, it couldn't be helped – I stand face to face with the 'Commander'.

With casual audacity, I even move a step away from the wall to make him aware of me. I don't do it to awaken his compassion but to mock myself, make myself an object of derision. I could have thrown myself in the gutter and asked the 'Commander' to walk over me, to trample on my face. I don't even say good evening to him.

Perhaps the 'Commander' sensed there was something wrong with me; he slowed down a little and I said to make him stop, 'I should have brought you something, but I haven't got round to it yet.'

'Yes?' he answers, enquiringly. 'So you haven't finished it?'

'No, I haven't managed to finish it.'

But now, with the 'Commander's' friendliness, my eyes are suddenly watering, and I hawk and cough furiously to toughen myself. The 'Commander' gives a snort; he stands looking at me.

'And do you have anything to live on in the meantime?' he says.

'No,' I answer, 'I suppose I don't. I haven't had anything to eat yet today, but—'

'God help us, man, that won't do; you just can't let yourself starve to death!' And he reaches for his pocket right away.

At this, my sense of shame awakens, I stagger up to the

wall again and hold onto it. I watch the 'Commander'
rummaging in his wallet but don't say anything. He hands
me a ten-krone note. He doesn't make a big fuss about it,
he simply gives me ten kroner. At the same time he repeats
that it wouldn't do for me to starve to death.

I stammered an objection and didn't accept the note
right away: I ought to feel ashamed . . . besides, it was
far too much. . . .

'Hurry up,' he says, looking at his watch. 'I've been
waiting for the train and now I hear it coming.'

I took the money. Paralysed with joy, I didn't say
another word, even forgetting to thank him.

'There's no need to feel embarrassed about it,' the
'Commander' says at last. 'You can always write for it,
you know.'

Then he left.

When he had gone a few steps I suddenly remembered
that I hadn't thanked the 'Commander' for his help. I tried
to overtake him but couldn't move fast enough, my legs
gave way and I was constantly on the point of falling on
my face. He got further and further away. Giving up the
attempt, I thought of shouting after him but didn't dare,
and when I finally took heart all the same and called once
or twice, he was already too far away – my voice had
grown too weak.

Left behind on the sidewalk, I followed him with my
eyes, crying quietly. Did you ever see anything like it! I
said to myself; he gave me ten kroner! I walked back
and placed myself where he had stood and imitated all
his movements. Then I held the note up to my moist eyes,
inspected it on both sides, and began to swear, hurling a

wild oath into the blue inane: there was no mistake about it, I was holding a ten-krone bill in my hand.

A while afterwards – perhaps a very long while, for it had grown fairly quiet everywhere by this time – I stood, strangely enough, in front of 11 Tomte Street. It was here I had swindled a coachman who had driven me once, and it was here I had walked straight through the house without being seen by anybody. After collecting myself for a moment and wondering, I went through the door for the second time, straight into 'Refreshments and Lodging for Travellers'. Here I asked to be put up for the night and was given a bed right away.

Tuesday.

Sunshine and calm weather, a wonderfully clear day. The snow was gone; gaiety and good cheer everywhere, happy faces, smiles and laughter. The jets of water rising from the fountains formed arcs that turned golden from the sun, bluish from the blue sky.

Around noon I left my lodging on Tomte Street, where I was still staying and doing fine on the 'Commander's' ten-krone bill, and went out. I was in exuberant spirits and loafed about all afternoon in the most crowded streets, observing the people. Before seven in the evening I took a stroll to St Olaf Place and peeped on the sly up at the windows of number 2. In an hour I would see her! I was caught up in a mild, delicious fear the whole time. What would happen? What should I say when she came down the stairs? Good evening, miss? Or just smile? I decided to settle for the smile. Of course I would make a deep bow to her.

I slunk away, a little ashamed at being so early, and wandered about on Karl Johan Street a while, keeping an eye on the University clock. When it turned eight I started up University Street again. On the way it occurred to me that I might be a few minutes late, and I pressed on as best I could. My foot was very sore, otherwise there was nothing the matter with me.

I posted myself near the fountain and caught my breath. I stood there for quite a while, looking up at the windows of number 2, but she didn't come. Well, I would wait, I wasn't in a hurry; perhaps she had been detained. I waited some more. I couldn't have dreamed the whole thing, could I? Fantasised that first meeting with her the night I was laid up with a fever? Perplexed, I began to think back and wasn't at all sure.

'Hmm!' came from behind me.

I heard this sound, and I also heard light footsteps nearby; but I didn't turn round, only stared up at the tall flight of steps before me.

Then came, 'Good evening!'

I forget to smile, don't even tip my hat right away, being greatly surprised to see her coming from that direction.

'Have you been waiting long?' she says, breathing rapidly after her walk.

'No, not at all, I only came a short while ago,' I answered. 'Besides, what would it matter if I had waited long? By the way, I thought you would be coming from another direction.'

'I took Mama to see some friends – Mama will be away this evening.'

'Is that so!' I said.

We had started walking now. A policeman stands on the corner looking at us.

'Where are we actually going?' she says, stopping.

'Wherever you want, just where you want.'

'Oh dear. But it's such a bore to decide that yourself.' Pause.

Then I say, just to say something, 'Your windows are dark, I see.'

'Yes!' she answers vivaciously. 'The maid is off this evening, too. So I'm home all alone.'

We are both looking up at the windows of number 2, as if neither of us had ever seen them before.

'Can we go up to your place then?' I say. 'I'll sit by the door the whole time if you want me to. . . .'

But I was now trembling with emotion and feeling very sorry I had been so brash. What if she became offended and walked away? What if I never got to see her again? Oh, that wretched suit I was wearing! I waited desperately for her answer.

'You certainly won't sit by the door,' she says.

We went up.

In the hallway, where it was dark, she took my hand and led me on. I didn't have to be so quiet, she said, I could very well talk. We came in. As she made a light – she didn't light a lamp but a candle – as she lighted this candle, she said with a little laugh, 'But now you mustn't look at me. Oh, I'm so ashamed! But I'll never do it again.'

'What won't you ever do again?'

'I'll never . . . oh, dear, God forbid . . . I'll never kiss you again.'

'You won't?' I said, and we both laughed. I stretched out my arms for her but she slid aside, slipping away on the other side of the table. We stood looking at each other a little while, with the candle between us.

Then she began to untie her veil and take off her hat, while her sparkling eyes were glued to me, watching my movements to keep me from catching her. I made another lunge forward, tripped on the carpet and fell; my sore foot refused to hold me up any longer. I got up, extremely embarrassed.

'My goodness, how red you became!' she said. 'Was it as clumsy as all that?'

'Yes, it was.'

We began running around afresh.

'You seem to be limping.'

'I may be limping a little – just a little, though.'

'The last time you had a sore finger, now you have a sore foot. You certainly have lots of troubles.'

'I was run over a bit the other day.'

'Run over? Drunk again, then? Good heavens, what a life you're leading, young man!' She threatened me with her forefinger and put up a serious face. 'Let's sit down!' she said. 'No, not there by the door. You're too shy. Over here – you there and I here, that's it. . . . Oh, shy people are such a bore! One has to say and do everything oneself, they don't help out with anything. For example, I wouldn't mind if you put your hand on the back of my chair right now, you could easily have dreamed up that much by yourself, couldn't you? Because if I say something like that, your eyes pop as if you don't quite believe me. Yes, it's really true, I've seen it several times, you're doing it now too. But don't try to tell me you are that modest when you dare come on. You were brazen enough that day when you were tipsy and followed me straight home, pestering me with your witticisms: "You're losing your book, miss! You're most certainly losing your book, miss!" Ha-ha-ha! Goodness, you ought to be ashamed of yourself!'

I sat looking at her with rapt attention. My heart was thumping, the blood coursing warmly through my veins. What a wonderful pleasure to be sitting in a human dwelling again, hear a clock ticking, and talk with a lively young girl instead of with myself!

'Why don't you say something?'

'Ah, how sweet you are!' I said. 'I'm sitting here getting fascinated by you, at this moment I'm thoroughly fascinated. I can't help it. You are the strangest person that . . . Sometimes your eyes are so radiant, I've never seen anything like it, they look like flowers. Eh? No, no, maybe not like flowers but . . . I'm madly in love with you, and it won't do me a bit of good. What's your name? Really, you must tell me what your name is. . . .'

'No, what's *your* name? Goodness, I almost forgot again! I was thinking all day yesterday that I must ask you. Well, that is, not *all* day yesterday, I certainly didn't think about you all day yesterday.'

'Do you know what I've called you? I have called you Ylajali. How do you like it? Such a gliding sound—'

'Ylajali?'

'Yes.'

'Is it a foreign language?'

'Hmm. No, it's not.'

'Well, it isn't ugly.'

After long negotiations we told each other our names. She sat down right beside me on the sofa and pushed the chair away with her foot. We began chatting anew.

'You have shaved, too, this evening,' she said. 'You look on the whole a little better than last time, but actually only a wee bit better; just don't you imagine . . . No, the last time you were really mean. On top of it all, you had a horrible rag around your finger. And in that condition you were dead set on going in somewhere to have a glass of wine with me. No, thank you.'

'So it was because of my wretched appearance that you refused to go with me, wasn't it?' I said.

'No,' she answered, dropping her eyes. 'Oh no, God knows it wasn't! I didn't even think of that.'

'Look,' I said. 'You imagine I can dress and live exactly as I please, don't you? But, you see, I can't do that. I'm very, very poor.'

She looked at me.

'You are?' she said.

'Yes, I am.'

Pause.

'Oh dear me, so am I,' she said with a brisk movement of her head.

Every one of her words intoxicated me, fell on my heart like drops of wine, though she was probably a perfectly average Kristiania girl, with her jargon, her bold little sallies, and her chatter. She delighted me with the way she had of tilting her head slightly sideways as she listened to me talk. And I could feel her breath full upon my face.

'Do you know,' I said, 'that . . . But promise you won't

get angry. . . . When I went to bed last night I put my arm out for you . . . like this . . . as if you were lying on it. And then I went to sleep.'

'Really? That was nice!' Pause. 'But you'd really have to be far away from me to do something like that, for otherwise—'

'You don't think I could do it otherwise?'

'No, I don't.'

'Oh yes, from me you can expect everything,' I said, puffing myself up. And I put my arm around her waist.

'I can?' she said, nothing more.

It annoyed and hurt me that she considered me too good. I threw out my chest, plucked up courage and grabbed her hand. But she pulled it quietly back and moved a little away from me. That was enough to kill my courage again. I felt ashamed and looked away, toward the window. Anyhow, I cut an all too sorry figure sitting there, I'd better not get any ideas. It would have been a different matter if I had met her while I still looked like a human being, in my heyday, when I had what it took to keep afloat. I felt very depressed.

'There, see!' she said. 'There you can see! All it takes to knock you over is a tiny frown, you look sheepish as soon as one moves a little away from you. . . .' She laughed impishly, her eyes completely closed, as if she herself couldn't stand being looked at.

'Well, I never!' I blurted out. 'Just you wait and see!' And I flung my arms lustily around her shoulders. Was the girl out of her mind? Did she take me for a complete innocent? Haw-haw, wouldn't I, though, by the living. . . . No one should say about me that I was backward on that score. What a little devil! If it was just a matter of pushing on, then . . .

As though I was good for much of anything!

She sat quite still, her eyes closed as before; neither of us spoke. I pressed her hard to me, squeezing her body against my breast, and she didn't say a word. I could hear our heartbeats, both hers and mine; they sounded like hoofbeats.

I kissed her.

I didn't know what I was doing any more, said some nonsense that she laughed at, whispered endearments against her mouth, stroked her cheek and kissed her again and again. I opened a button or two in her bodice and glimpsed her breasts underneath, white, round breasts that peeked out like two sweet miracles behind her underlinen.

'May I see?' I say, trying some more buttons, eager to enlarge the opening. But I can't get anywhere with the lower buttons, my emotion is too strong and, besides, her bodice is tighter there. 'May I see just a little . . . a little . . . ?'

She winds her arm around my neck, quite slowly, tenderly; her breath blows directly on my face from her red, quivering nostrils. With the other hand she begins to undo the buttons herself, one by one. She laughs bashfully, a short laugh, and glances up at me several times to see whether I notice she's afraid. She unties the bands and unhooks her corset, rapt and apprehensive. And my coarse hands fiddle with these buttons and bands.

To distract my attention from what she is doing, she

runs her left hand over my shoulder and says, 'What a lot of loose hair you've got here!'

'Yes,' I reply, trying to press my mouth onto her bosom. At this moment she lies with her clothes completely open. Suddenly she seems to change her mind, as though she feels she has gone too far. She covers herself again and sits up a little. To hide her embarrassment over her unbuttoned clothes, she starts talking once more about all the dead hair on my shoulders.

'How come you're losing so much hair?'

'Don't know.'

'You drink too much, of course, and perhaps . . . Goodness, I won't even say it! You ought to be ashamed of yourself! I wouldn't have believed it of you, no, never! To think that you, who are so young, should already be losing your hair! . . . Now you'd better tell me what sort of life you're leading. I'm sure it's awful! But only the truth, mind you, no quibbles! Anyway, I'll know from your face if you try to hide something. So, go on and tell me!'

Oh, how tired I was! How much I'd rather sit still looking at her than putting on an act and taking a lot of trouble over all these moves. I was good for nothing, I'd turned into a wet sock.

'Come on, will you!' she said.

I seized the opportunity and told her everything, and I told nothing but the truth. I didn't make anything worse than it was, it wasn't my intention to arouse her compassion. I even said that I had walked off with five kroner one evening.

She was listening agape, pale, frightened, her shining

eyes quite troubled. I wanted to put it right again, to dispel the sad impression I had made, and so I pulled myself together. 'Anyway, it's over now, there's no question of such doings any more; I'm saved now. . . .'

But she was very crestfallen. 'Lord help me!' she said, just that, and was silent. She said this at short intervals and then was silent again, each time. 'Lord help me!'

I began joking, poked her in the side to tickle her and lifted her up to my breast. She had buttoned her dress again, and that annoyed me. Why should she button her dress? Was I less worthy now, in her eyes, than if I had only myself to blame for my hair falling out, because of unbridled living? Would she have thought better of me if I had turned myself into a roué? . . . No nonsense now! It was only a matter of pushing on! And if it was only a matter of pushing on, then I was the right man.

I had to try once more.

I laid her down, simply laid her down on the sofa. She struggled, not much though, and looked astonished.

'No! . . . What do you want?' she said.

'What do I want?'

'No! . . . Why, no . . .!'

'Oh yes, oh yes . . .!'

'No, d'you hear!' she cried. And she added these cutting words, 'Why, I believe you're insane!'

Startled into leaving off for a moment, I said, 'You don't mean that!'

'Oh yes, you look so strange! And that morning when you were following me – so you weren't really drunk that time?'

'No. But I wasn't hungry either then, you know; I had just eaten.'

'So much the worse.'

'Would you rather I had been drunk?'

'Yes . . . Oh, I'm so scared of you! Good God, can't you let go of me!'

I thought it over. No, I couldn't let go, I would lose too much that way. No damn nonsense on a sofa at this time of night! Ha, the sort of excuses they dreamed up at such a moment! As if I didn't know it was all nothing but bashfulness! How naive could I be? So, quiet now! No nonsense!

She fought me off vigorously, oddly enough, far too vigorously simply to arise from bashfulness. I knocked the candle over by mistake, so it went out. She fought back desperately, even gave out a little whimper.

'No, not that, not that! If you want to, I'd let you kiss my bosom instead. Please, please!'

I stopped immediately. Her words sounded so frightened, so helpless that I was touched to the quick. She meant to offer me compensation by allowing me to kiss her bosom! How beautiful, beautiful and naive! I could have fallen on my knees before her.

'But my dear!' I said, quite confused. 'I don't understand . . . I really can't understand what sort of game you're playing. . . .'

She got up and lighted the candle again with trembling hands. I was left on the sofa doing nothing. What would happen now? I felt extremely ill at ease.

She glanced at the wall, at the clock, and gave a start.

'Oh, the maid will be home soon!' she said. This was the first thing she said.

I understood the hint and stood up. She reached for her coat as if to put it on but changed her mind, let it lie where it was and went over to the fireplace. She was pale and grew more and more restless. So it shouldn't look like she was throwing me out, I said, 'Was your father a military man?' At the same time I got ready to leave.

'Yes, he was. How did you know?'

'I didn't, it just occurred to me.'

'That's odd.'

'Well, yes.' There were certain places I went where I would get hunches. 'Hee-hee, it's part of my madness, you know. . . .'

She looked up quickly but didn't answer. I felt my presence was painful to her and wanted to get it over with. I went to the door. She wouldn't kiss me any more, would she? Not even give me her hand? I was waiting.

'Are you going now?' she said, still standing quietly over by the fireplace.

I didn't answer. I felt humiliated and confused and looked at her without speaking. Oh, what a mess I'd made! It didn't seem to affect her that I stood there ready to go; all at once she was completely lost to me, and I searched for something to say to her for goodbye, some deep, weighty word that would cut into her and maybe impress her a little. But in the teeth of my firm resolve, hurt instead of being proud and cold, uneasy and offended, I just started talking about trivia. The cutting word didn't come, I behaved very thoughtlessly. It was just claptrap and rhetoric over again.

Why couldn't she just tell me, in no uncertain terms, to leave? I asked. Yes, yes, why not? There was no need to feel embarrassed about it. Instead of reminding me that the maid would soon be home, she could simply have said the following: Now you must get lost, because I'm going to pick up my mother, and I don't want to be seen walking down the street with you. So, that was not what she'd been thinking? Oh yes, that was what she'd been thinking, all right, I understood that at once. It took so little to put me on the track; just the way she had reached for her coat and then left it where it was had convinced me immediately. As I had said before, I had a knack for hunches. And it might not be that crazy either, not really—.

'But good heavens, can't you forgive me for that one word! It just slipped out,' she cried. But she still stood motionless and didn't come over to me.

I was unrelenting and went on. I stood there jabbering away, having the unpleasant feeling that I was boring her, that not a single one of my words hit home, and yet I didn't stop. One could, after all, be quite a sensitive person even if one wasn't insane, I said; there were natures that fed on mere nothings and died from a harsh word. I gave her to understand that I had such a nature. The fact of the matter was that my poverty had sharpened certain aptitudes in me to such a degree that it got me into outright trouble – 'Yes, I assure you, outright trouble, I'm sorry to say.' But it also had its advantages, it helped me in certain situations. The intelligent poor individual was a much finer observer than the intelligent rich one. The poor individual looks around him at every step, listens suspiciously to every word he hears from the people he meets; thus, every step he takes presents a problem, a task, for his thoughts and feelings. He is alert and sensitive, he is experienced, his soul has been burned. . . .

I talked at length about these burns which my soul had suffered. But the longer I talked, the more anxious she became; finally she said 'Oh, my God!' in despair a couple of times, wringing her hands. I could see quite well that I was torturing her, and I didn't want to torture her but did so anyway. At last I thought I had managed to tell her the broad essentials of what I had to say. I was moved by her despairing look and cried:

'I'm leaving, I'm leaving! Can't you see I have my hand on the latch already? Goodbye! Goodbye! I tell you. You could at least answer when I say goodbye twice, all ready to leave. I don't even ask to see you again, because it would cause you pain. But tell me, Why didn't you leave me alone? What have I ever done to you? I didn't get in your way, did I? Why do you suddenly turn away from me, as if you don't know me any longer? You have plucked me thoroughly clean, made me more wretched than I've ever been. But, good God, I'm not insane. You know very well if you stop and think that there's nothing wrong with me now. So, come here and give me your hand! Or let me come to you. Will you? I won't do you any harm, I'll just kneel before you a moment, kneel on the floor right there, in front of you, for just a moment; may I? No, no, then I won't do it, I can see you're scared, I won't, I *won't* do it, do you hear? Good God, why are you getting so frightened? I'm standing still after all, I'm not budging. I would've kneeled down on the carpet for a minute, right there, on that red spot near your feet.

But you got scared, I could tell by your eyes right away that you got scared, and so I stood still. I didn't move one step while I was asking you to let me, did I? I stood quite motionless, like now, when I'm showing you the place where I would've kneeled before you, over there on that red rose in the carpet. I'm not even pointing with my finger, I'm not pointing at all, I'm holding off not to alarm you; I'm just nodding and looking over there, like this! You understand very well which rose I mean, but you won't allow me to kneel there; you're afraid of me and don't dare come near me. I don't understand how you could have the heart to call me insane. You don't believe that any longer, do you? There was a time last summer, long ago, when I was insane; I was working too hard and forgot to go to dinner on time when I had a lot to think about. It happened day after day; I ought to have remembered but constantly forgot about it. I swear to God, it's true! May God never let me out of this place alive if I'm lying! So, you see, you're doing me an injustice. It wasn't out of need that I did it; I have credit, lots of credit, at Ingebret's and Gravesen's. Also, I often had plenty of money in my pocket, and yet I didn't buy any food because I forgot to. Do you hear? You don't say a word, you don't answer me, you don't budge from the fireplace, you just stand there waiting for me to go. . . .'

She came quickly over to me and held out her hand. I looked at her full of distrust. Was she doing this freely, with a light heart? Or was she doing it just to get rid of me? She put her arm around my neck, tears in her eyes. I just stood and looked at her. She offered me her mouth but I couldn't believe her, it was bound to be a sacrifice on her part, a means of getting it over with.

She said something, it sounded to me like, 'I love you anyway!' She said it very softly and indistinctly, I may not have heard it correctly, perhaps she didn't say exactly those words. But she threw herself passionately on my neck, held both arms around my neck a little while, even raised herself on tiptoe to reach well up, and stood thus.

Afraid that she was forcing herself to show me this tenderness, I merely said, 'How beautiful you are now!'

That was all I said. I stepped back, bumped against the door and walked out backward. She was left standing inside.

Part Four

Winter had come, a raw and wet winter with hardly any snow, a dark and foggy everlasting night without a single fresh gust of wind all week long. The street lamps were lit almost all day, and yet people kept running into one another in the fog. All sounds, the peal of the church bells, the harness bells on the cab horses, people's voices, the hoofbeats – everything came through so muffled in the heavy air, as though it was buried. Week after week went by and the weather remained the same.

I was still staying down in the Vaterland section.

I became more and more attached to this tavern, this rooming house for travellers, where I had been allowed to stay despite being so down-and-out. My money had been used up long ago, but I continued to come and go in the house, as if I were entitled to it and belonged there. The landlady hadn't said a word yet, but it worried me nonetheless that I couldn't pay her. Three weeks went by in this way.

I had resumed my writing several days ago, but I was no longer able to come up with anything I was satisfied with; I had no luck at all any more, though I worked very hard and kept trying at all times. It was no use whatever I tried, my luck was gone.

I was sitting in a room on the second floor, the best guest room, when I made these attempts. I had been left undisturbed up there since that first evening, when I had money and could pay up. I kept hoping all along I might finally put together an article about something or other, so I could pay for my room and whatever else I owed; that was why I was working so hard. In particular, I had started a piece for which I had high expectations, an allegory about a fire in a bookshop, a profound idea that I would take the utmost pains to work out and bring to the 'Commander' as an installment on my debt. Then the 'Commander' would realise he had helped a real talent this time; I had no doubt he would realise that, I just had to wait for the inspiration to come. And why shouldn't the inspiration come, even very soon? There was nothing the matter with me any more; I got a little food from my landlady every day, a few sandwiches morning and evening, and my nervousness was all but gone. I no longer had rags around my hands when I wrote, and I could look down into the street from my second-floor windows without getting dizzy. I was doing much better in every way, and I was actually beginning to wonder why I hadn't finished my allegory yet. I couldn't understand what the explanation was.

One day I was at last to get an inkling of how weak I had really become, how sluggishly and ineptly my brain was working. That day my landlady came upstairs with a bill which she asked me to look at. There must be something wrong with the bill, she said, it didn't tally with her own books; but she hadn't been able to find the mistake.

I set about adding it up; my landlady sat directly opposite, watching me. I added up the twenty items first once down, and found the total to be correct, then once up and came again to the same result. I looked at the woman sitting right in front of me, waiting for my word; I noticed immediately that she was pregnant, it didn't escape my attention though I looked anything but closely at her.

'The sum is correct,' I said.

'Check every item, will you?' she answered. 'It can't be that much, I'm sure it can't.'

I began to review every item: 2 loaves of bread at 25 each; 1 lamp glass, 18; soap, 20; butter, 32. . . . No clever head was needed to go through these rows of numbers, this piddling huckster's bill which wasn't the least bit complicated, and I tried honestly to find the mistake the woman was talking about, but couldn't. After grappling with these figures for a few minutes, I felt, unhappily, that everything started spinning in my head; I no longer distinguished between debit and credit but mixed it all up. Finally, I froze in my tracks all of a sudden at the following item: $1^{10}/16$ pounds of cheese at 32 a pound. My brain was completely stumped, I stared stupidly down at that cheese and couldn't get anywhere.

'I'm damned if I ever saw such a screwed-up way of putting things!' I said desperately. 'Here it says flatly, God help me, ten-sixteenths of cheese. Ha-ha, who ever heard of anything like that! Here, see for yourself!'

'Yes,' the matron answered, 'that's the way it's usually

written. It's the clove cheese. Oh yes, that's correct! Ten-sixteenths, that's ten ounces—'

'That much I understand!' I broke in, though in fact I didn't understand a thing any more.

I tried again to tackle this little sum, which I could have added up in a minute a few months ago. Perspiring heavily, I applied myself to these enigmatic figures with all my might, blinking my eyes thoughtfully as if I were studying the matter real hard; but I had to give up. Those ten ounces of cheese finished me completely; it was as though something had snapped in my head.

However, to give the impression that I was still working on my computations, I moved my lips and spoke some number aloud every now and then, all the while sliding further and further down the bill as if I were making steady progress and getting close to the finish. The matron was waiting. Finally I said, 'Well, now I have gone through it from beginning to end, and there is really no mistake, as far as I can see.'

'There isn't?' the woman replied. 'There isn't, well!' But it was quite apparent that she didn't believe me. And suddenly her speech seemed to take on a touch of contempt, a slightly indifferent tone which I hadn't heard in her voice before. She said that maybe I wasn't used to figuring with sixteenths; she also said she would have to turn to someone who was up on things to get the bill properly checked. She didn't say all this in any hurtful manner, to put me to shame, but thoughtfully and seriously. When she got to the door and was about to leave, she said, without looking at me, 'Excuse me for taking up your time!'

She left.

Shortly afterward the door opened again and my land-lady came in once more; she could hardly have gone further than the hallway before turning around.

'By the way,' she said, 'you mustn't be offended, but you do owe me some money by now, don't you? It was three weeks ago yesterday since you came, wasn't it? I reckoned it was, anyway. It's not easy to manage with such a big family, so I'm afraid I can't let anyone stay here on credit—'

I stopped her.

'I'm working on an article, as I mentioned to you before,' I said, 'and as soon as it's finished you'll get your money. There's no need to worry.'

'But you won't ever finish that article, will you?'

'You think so? I may feel inspired to write tomorrow, or maybe even tonight; it's not at all impossible that the inspiration will come sometime tonight, and then my article will be finished in a quarter of an hour, at the most. You see, it's not the same with my work as with other people's; I can't just sit down and get so much done every day, I have to wait for the right moment. And nobody can tell the day or the hour when the spirit will come upon him. It must take its course.'

My landlady left. But her confidence in me seemed greatly shaken.

As soon as I was alone, I sprang up and started tearing my hair in despair. No, there wasn't the least hope for me, no hope at all! My brain was bankrupt! Had I turned into an utter idiot, since I couldn't even work out the price of a piece of clove cheese any more? But then, could I have lost my wits as long as I was asking myself questions like that? On top of it all, hadn't I made the crystal-clear observation in the midst of my efforts with the bill that my landlady was pregnant? I had no basis for knowing that, nobody had told me anything about it, nor did it occur to me haphazardly – I saw it with my own eyes and I understood it immediately, in a moment of desperation at that, when I was grappling with sixteenths! How was I to explain that?

I walked to the window and looked out; my window faced Vognmand Street. Some children were playing on the pavement below, poorly dressed children in the middle of a poverty-stricken street. They were tossing an empty bottle back and forth amid loud yells. A moving van rolled slowly by; it must have been an evicted family, since they were moving at this unusual time of year. This thought came to me immediately. The van was loaded with bedding and furniture, worm-eaten beds and chests of drawers, red-painted chairs with three legs, mats, scrap iron, tin articles. A little girl, a mere child, a downright ugly brat with a runny nose, was sitting on top of the load, holding on with her poor blue hands to keep from falling off. She sat on a bunch of ghastly, wet mattresses that had been slept on by children, and looked down at the small fry tossing the empty bottle among themselves.

I was watching all this and hadn't the least difficulty understanding what was going on. While I stood there at the window observing it, I could also hear my landlady's maid singing in the kitchen, right beside my room; I knew the tune she was singing and was listening on purpose to hear if she would make a mistake. I said to myself that no idiot could have done all this; I was, thank God, as much in my senses as anyone.

Suddenly I saw two of the children in the street leaping up and starting to wrangle, two small boys; I knew one of them, my landlady's son. I open the window to hear what they are saying to each other, and instantly a flock of children crowd together under my window and look up wishfully. What were they waiting for? Something to be thrown down? Dried-up flowers, bones, cigar stubs, something or other they could chew on or amuse themselves with? They looked up at my window with infinitely wistful eyes, their faces blue with cold. In the meantime the two small enemies continue to shout at each other. Words swarm out of their childish mouths like big clammy monsters, horrible nicknames, gutter language, sailors' swearwords which they had probably picked up down at the docks. They're both so engrossed in this that they don't notice my landlady, who comes rushing out to learn what's going on.

'Why,' her son explains, 'he grabbed me by the weasand, it took me a long time to get my wind back.' Then, turning toward the little malefactor, who is laughing maliciously at him, he flies into a rage and yells, 'Go and fry in hell, you Chaldean beast! That a filthy bastard like you should dare grab people by the throat! By golly, I'll—'

And the mother, this pregnant woman who dominates the whole length of this narrow street with her belly, answers the ten-year-old, seizing him by the arm to pull him along, 'Ssh! Shut your trap! So you swear too, do you? You're shooting your mouth off like someone who's spent years in a whorehouse! Now, get yourself inside!'

185

'No, I won't!'
'Oh yes, you will!'
'No, I won't!'

I stand at the window and see the mother's anger rising. This ghastly scene upsets me terribly, I cannot take it any longer and call down to the boy to come up to me a moment. I call twice just to distract them, trying to break it up; my last call is very loud and the mother, bewildered, turns around and looks up at me. But she regains her composure on the spot, looks at me brazenly, downright arrogantly, and then marches off with a reproachful remark to her son. Talking loudly for my benefit, she says to him, 'You ought to be ashamed of yourself, letting people see how bad you are!'

In all that I observed in this way, there was nothing, not even a tiny incidental circumstance, that escaped me. My attention was most alert, every little thing was sensitively picked up, and I had my own ideas about these matters as they occurred. So there couldn't possibly be anything wrong with my sanity. As things were, how could there possibly be anything the matter with it?

Now, look here, I said all of a sudden, you have been bothering yourself about your sanity long enough, making yourself anxious on that score; now let's put a stop to these tomfooleries! Is it a sign of insanity to perceive and understand all things as accurately as you do? On my word, you almost make me laugh at yourself; it does have its humorous side, you know. In short, everyone gets stuck once in a while, and precisely in the simplest things. It doesn't mean anything, it's pure chance. As I've said, I'm only a hairsbreadth away from having a good laugh at you. As far as that grocery bill is concerned, those piddling ten-sixteenths of a poor man's cheese, I might call it – hee-hee, a cheese with cloves and pepper in it – as far as this ridiculous cheese is concerned, the very best among us might have been stupefied by that. The very smell of that cheese could finish a man. . . . And I held all clove cheese up to the most vicious ridicule. . . . No, give me something edible! I said. Give me, if you please, ten-sixteenths of good creamery butter! That's something else!

I laughed frantically at my own cracks, finding them terribly funny. There was really nothing wrong with me any more, I was in my right mind.

My gaiety kept rising as I paced the floor talking to myself; I laughed aloud and felt mighty glad. It really looked as though all I needed was this brief happy hour, this moment of truly carefree delight without a worry on the horizon, to get my head in working order. I sat down at the table and started busying myself with my allegory. It went very well, better than it had in a long while. It didn't go fast, but I thought the little I accomplished was altogether first-rate. Also, I worked for about an hour without getting tired.

I am right now at a very important point in my allegory about a fire in a bookshop. It seemed to me so important that everything else I had written counted for nothing as compared to this point. I was about to express, in a truly profound way, the idea that it wasn't books that were burning, it was brains, human brains, and I wanted to make a veritable Bartholomew's Night out of these burning brains. Suddenly my door was opened in great haste and my landlady came barging in. She strode to the middle of the room, without even stopping on the threshold.

I gave a little hoarse cry; indeed, I felt as though I had received a blow.

'What?' she said. 'I thought you said something. We've got a new arrival and need this room for him. You can sleep downstairs with us tonight, you'll have your own bed there too.' And before I had managed to answer her, she began quite casually to gather up my papers on the table, messing them all up.

My happy mood was blown away, I was angry and desperate and got up at once. I let her clear the table without opening my mouth; I didn't utter a word. She handed me all the papers.

There was nothing else I could do, I had to vacate the room. And so this precious moment, too, was spoiled! I met the new arrival on the stairs, a young man with big blue anchors traced on the backs of his hands. Behind him came a stevedore with a sea chest on his shoulder. The stranger was evidently a sailor, hence just a casual overnight guest; he would hardly occupy my room for any length of time. Perhaps, too, I would be lucky tomorrow, when the man was gone, and get one of my good moments again. All I needed now was a five-minute inspiration, and my work about the fire would be finished. So I'd better put up with my lot.

I hadn't been inside the family's apartment before, this one room in which they were all staying night and day – husband, wife, the wife's father, and four children. The maid lived in the kitchen, where she also slept at night. I approached the door very reluctantly and knocked. Nobody answered, but I could hear talk inside.

The husband didn't say a word when I entered, didn't even answer my greeting; he merely gave me an indifferent glance as if I didn't concern him. Anyway, he was playing cards with a person I had seen down at the docks, a porter who answered to the name 'Pane o' Glass'. An infant lay prattling to itself over in the bed, and the old man, the landlady's father, sat hunched up on a sofa bed, his head bent over his hands as though he had a pain in his chest or stomach. His hair was nearly white, and in his hunched-up position he looked like a humped insect pricking up its ears for something.

'I'm sorry, but I've come to ask for a place to stay down here tonight,' I said to the husband.

'Did my wife say so?' he asked.

'Yes. A new man has moved into my room.'

To this the husband made no reply; he addressed himself to his cards again.

This man would sit like that day after day, playing cards with anyone who happened to drop in, playing for nothing, just to kill time and have something in his hands while it lasted. Beyond that he did nothing, stirring no more than his lazy limbs felt inclined to, while his wife trudged up and down the stairs, bustled about everywhere, and saw to the business of getting patrons for the house. She had also made contacts with dockers and porters, whom she paid a certain fee for every new lodger they brought her, and she often gave these dockers shelter for the night. This time it was 'Pane o' Glass' who had brought the new guest.

Two of the children came in, a pair of small girls with thin, freckled, sluttish faces; they were quite wretchedly clad. Shortly afterward the landlady came in too. I asked her where she wanted to put me up for the night, and she answered curtly that I could sleep here, together with the others, or on the sofa bed in the hall, just as I pleased. As she was giving me this answer, she walked around the room, busying herself with various things which she put in order, and she didn't even look at me.

My heart sank at her answer; I stood by the door trying to look small, even pretending I was perfectly happy to trade rooms with someone else for the night. I put on a friendly face on purpose, so as not to provoke her and perhaps get thrown out of the house altogether. I said, 'Oh well, I'll manage somehow,' and was silent.

She was still scurrying around the room.

'While I think of it, I must tell you that I simply can't afford to let people have board and room on credit,' she said. 'I have told you this before, remember.'

'But, please, it's only a matter of a couple of days, till my article gets finished,' I answered. 'Then I'll gladly give you an extra five-krone bill, yes, very gladly.'

But she obviously had no faith in my article, I could see that. And I couldn't start acting proud and leave the house only because of a slight insult. I knew what awaited me if I marched off.

A few days went by.

I was still staying downstairs with the family, since it was too cold in the hall where there was no stove; and at night I slept on the floor in the family room. The stranger was still living in my room and didn't seem minded to move out very soon. Anyway, around noon the landlady came in and said that the sailor had paid up for a whole month in advance. Incidentally, he was going to take his mate's examination before leaving, that was why he was staying in town. Hearing this, I understood that my room was now lost to me for good.

I went out into the hall and sat down; if I should be lucky enough to get anything written, it would have to be here, in the stillness, despite everything. I was no longer occupied with my allegory; I had a new idea, a really splendid plan: I was going to compose a one-act drama, 'The Sign of the Cross', on a subject from the Middle Ages. In particular, the central character was fully worked out in my mind – a gorgeous fanatical whore who had sinned in the temple, not out of weakness or lust, but from a hatred of heaven, had sinned at the very foot of the altar, with the altar cloth under her head, simply from a voluptuous contempt of heaven.

I became more and more obsessed by this character as the hours went by. She stood vividly alive before my eyes at last, exactly the way I wanted to portray her. Her body was to be misshapen and repulsive: tall, very skinny and rather dark, with long legs that showed through her skirts at every step she took. She would also have big, protruding ears. In short, she would not be easy on the eye, barely tolerable to look at. What interested me about her was her wonderful shamelessness, the desperate excess of premeditated sin that she had committed. I was actually too much taken up with her, my brain was downright swollen with this peculiar monstrosity of a human being. I worked for two whole hours at a stretch on my play.

When I had done about ten pages, or perhaps twelve, often with great difficulty, at times with long intervals during which I wrote to no avail and had to tear up my sheets, I was tired, quite numb with cold and weariness, and I got up and went out into the street. For the last half hour I had also been disturbed by the bawling of children coming from the family room, so I couldn't have written any more just then anyway. I therefore took a long walk along the Drammen Road and stayed away till the evening, all the while pondering how I should continue my play. Before I got home that day, the following had happened to me:

I was standing outside a shoemaker's shop at the bottom of Karl Johan Street, just short of Jærnbanetorvet Square. God knows why I had stopped outside this particular shoemaker's shop. I kept looking in through the window from where I stood, though I wasn't thinking I needed a pair of shoes just then; my thoughts were far away, in other parts of the world. A flock of people talking together walked past behind my back, and I heard nothing of what was said. Then a loud voice says, 'Good evening.'

It was the 'Maiden' who greeted me.

'Good evening,' I answered, absently. Actually, I looked at the 'Maiden' a moment before recognising him.

'Well, how are you doing?' he asked.

'Oh, I'm fine . . . as usual.'

'Come, tell me,' he said, 'are you still at Christie's?'

'Christie's?'

'I seem to remember you told me once that you were bookkeeper at Christie's, the merchant.'

'Ah, yes. No, that's over. It was impossible to work with that man; it came to a halt by itself fairly soon.'

'Why?'

'Oh, I happened to make a slip of the pen one day, and so—'

'Meaning forgery?'

'Forgery?' There stood the 'Maiden' asking me point-blank if I had committed forgery. He even put his question quickly and interestedly. I looked at him, felt deeply insulted and didn't answer.

'Good heavens, man, that could happen to the best of us,' he said, to comfort me. He still believed that I had committed forgery.

'What is it that, good heavens, can happen to the best of us?' I asked. 'Committing forgery? Listen, my friend, do you really believe I could have done such a dastardly thing? I?'

'But dear me, I thought you said quite clearly . . .'

I tossed my head, turned away from the 'Maiden' and looked down the street. My eyes fell upon a red dress that was approaching us, a woman walking with a man. If I hadn't been having exactly this conversation with the 'Maiden', I wouldn't have been hurt by his crude suspicion, and if I hadn't made precisely this toss of my head and turned away offended, this red dress might have passed me by without my noticing. What business was it of mine anyway? Even if it were the dress of Miss Nagel, the lady-in-waiting, what concern was it of mine?

The 'Maiden' was talking, trying to make up for his

mistake. I didn't pay any attention to him, my eyes were all the time riveted on this red dress coming on up the street. A flutter went through my breast, a delicate, gliding stab. I whispered inwardly, without moving my lips, Ylajali!

Now the 'Maiden' too turned around, discovered the pair, the lady and the gentleman, bowed to them and followed them with his eyes. I didn't bow, or perhaps I did. The red dress glided up Karl Johan Street and disappeared.

'Who was the one with her?' the 'Maiden' asked.

'The "Duke". Didn't you see? The "Duke", so-called. Did you know the lady?'

'Yes, just barely. Didn't you?'

'No,' I answered.

'It seemed to me you made such a deep bow.'

'Did I?'

'Ha, didn't you, though!' the 'Maiden' said. 'How odd! And she looked only at you, all along.'

'Where do you know her from?' I asked.

He didn't really know her. It dated back to an evening last autumn. It was late, they had been out together, three merry souls, had just left the Grand Café when they met this person walking alone near Cammermeyer's and talked to her. She had brushed them off at first, but one of the merry souls, a man who feared neither fire nor water, asked her point-blank if he could walk her home. As God was his witness, he wouldn't touch a hair on her head, as the saying goes, only walk her to her door to make certain she got home safely, otherwise he wouldn't have a moment's rest all night. He talked endlessly as they walked on, had one wild idea after another, called himself Waldemar Atterdag and passed himself off as a photographer. At last she couldn't help laughing at this merry soul, who had refused to be impressed by her coldness, and the upshot was that he went with her.

'Well, what came of it?' I asked with bated breath.

'Came of it? Ah, forget it. She's a lady.'

We were silent a moment, both the 'Maiden' and I.

'That was the "Duke", was it? I'll be damned! So that's what he looks like!' he then said, pensively. 'But if she keeps company with that man, I won't answer for her.'

I was still silent. Yes, the 'Duke' would walk off with her, of course! Well and good! What business was it of mine? I didn't give a hang about her, or about all her charms, not a hang! And I tried to comfort myself by thinking the worst possible things about her, took downright pleasure in rolling her in the mud. The only thing that annoyed me was that I had taken off my hat to the pair – if, indeed, I had done so. Why should I take off my hat to such people? I no longer cared for her, not at all; she wasn't the least attractive any more, she had lost her good looks – bloody hell, how she had faded! It might very well be she had looked only at me; it wouldn't surprise me, perhaps remorse was beginning to gnaw at her. But that was no reason why I had to go down on my knees and bow to her like a fool, especially since she had faded so suspiciously lately. The 'Duke' was quite welcome to keep her, much good might she do him! A day might come when I would take it into my head to walk proudly past her, without even glancing in her direction. I might venture to do this even if she looked hard at me, and was wearing a blood-red dress to boot! I might do it, all right. Ha-ha, what a triumph that would be! If I knew myself at all, I would be able to finish my play in the course of the night, and within a week I would have brought the young lady to her knees. With her charms and all, hee-hee, with all her charms. . . .

'Goodbye,' I said curtly.

But the 'Maiden' held me back. He asked, 'So what are you doing these days?'

'Doing? I'm writing, of course. What else should I be doing? That's how I make my living, after all. At the moment I'm working on a great drama, "The Sign of the Cross", with a theme from the Middle Ages.'

'I'll be damned!' the 'Maiden' said, sincerely. 'Well, if you can carry it off—'

'I have no great worries on that score,' I answered. 'In a week or so I should think you'll have heard from me, one and all.'

Having said this, I left.

When I got home I went at once to my landlady and asked for a lamp. It was very important to me to have this lamp; I wouldn't go to bed tonight, my play was churning in my head, and I firmly hoped I could write a good portion of it before morning. I presented my request to the matron very humbly, noticing that she made a sour face because I came into the living room again. I had almost finished a remarkable play, I said, only a couple of scenes were missing; and I hinted that it might be presented in some theatre or other before I knew it. If she would just do me this great favour, then . . .

But the matron didn't have a lamp. She thought for a

moment, but couldn't remember having a lamp anywhere. If I cared to wait until twelve o'clock, maybe I could have the kitchen lamp. Why didn't I buy myself a candle?

I was silent. I didn't have ten øre to buy a candle, and she probably knew that. Needless to say, I would come to grief again! The maid, as it happened, was downstairs with us; she was simply sitting in the living room and was *not* in the kitchen, so the lamp up there wasn't even lit. I stood considering all this but said no more.

Suddenly the maid says to me, 'I thought I saw you leaving the Palace a little while ago. Did you go to a dinner party there?' Then she laughed aloud at her own joke.

I sat down and took out my papers, thinking I would try and do something here for the time being, right where I sat. I held the papers on my knees, staring continually at the floor so as not to be distracted by anything; but it wasn't any use, nothing was, I couldn't budge. The landlady's two little girls came in and raised a rumpus with the cat, a strange sick cat with hardly any hair on it. When they blew into its eyes, they watered, and the water trickled down its nose. The landlord and a couple of other individuals sat at the table playing *cent et un*. Only the wife was busy as usual, sewing something. She saw quite well that I couldn't write anything in the midst of this confusion, but she didn't bother herself with me any more; she had even smiled when the maid asked if I had been to a dinner party. The whole house had become hostile to me; it was as though I needed only the ignominy of having to turn over my room to someone else to be treated like an outright intruder. Even the maid, that little, flat-chested, brown-eyed slut with a fringe, made fun of me, when I got my sandwiches in the evening. She was constantly asking where I used to take my dinner, since she had never seen me picking my teeth outside the Grand Hotel. It was obvious that she knew all about my miserable plight and took pleasure in showing me she did.

Suddenly absorbed by all this, I cannot find a single line of dialogue for my play. I try again and again but in vain; my head begins to buzz eerily and in the end I give up. I stick the papers in my pocket and look up. The maid is sitting right in front of me and I look at her, look at that narrow back and those drooping shoulders, which weren't even quite grown-up yet. What business did she have to lay into me? Even supposing I had come out of the Palace, so what? Could it have harmed her? She had laughed saucily at me these last few days whenever I had the bad luck to stumble on the stairs or get caught on a nail, tearing my coat. And only yesterday she had gathered up my drafts, which I had thrown aside in the hall – she had stolen these scrapped fragments of my play and read them aloud in the family room, making fun of them in front of everybody just to amuse herself at my expense. I had never molested her and couldn't remember ever having asked her for a favour. On the contrary, I made up my own bed on the floor in the evening, so as not to give her any trouble with it. She made fun of me also because my hair was falling out. It was floating around in the washbasin in the morning, and she made merry over it. My shoes were in quite bad shape by now, especially the one that had been run over by the baker's van, and she also made jokes about them. 'God bless you and your shoes!' she would say; 'look at them, they're as big as doghouses!' She was right about my shoes being worn-down, but I just couldn't get myself another pair at the moment.

As I sat there recalling all this, wondering about the maid's blatant malice, the little girls had begun to tease the old greybeard over in the bed. They were both hopping around him, totally absorbed by their activities. They had each found a straw, which they were sticking into his ears. I watched this a while without meddling. The old man didn't lift a finger to defend himself; he merely looked at his tormentors with furious eyes each time they made a stab at him, and shook his head to free himself when the straws were already stuck in his ears.

I became more and more exasperated by this sight and couldn't take my eyes off it. The father looked up from his cards and laughed at the small fry; he also called the attention of his partners to what was going on. Why didn't the old fellow budge? Why didn't he push the children away with his arms? I took a step toward the bed.

'Leave them alone! Leave them alone! He's paralysed,' the landlord cried.

For fear of being turned out as night was coming on, positively afraid of arousing the man's displeasure by interfering with these goings-on, I stepped back to my old place without a word and kept quiet. Why should I risk my lodging and my sandwiches by sticking my nose into the family's squabbles? No tomfooleries, now, for the sake of a half-dead greybeard! I stood there feeling deliciously hard, like flint.

The little scamps didn't stop their harassment. Annoyed that the old man wouldn't hold his head still, they also stabbed at his eyes and nostrils. He stared at them with a steely glint in his eyes without saying a word, and he couldn't move his arms. Suddenly he lifted the upper part of his body and spat into the face of one of the little girls; he lifted himself once more and aimed a jet at the other too, but missed. Then I saw the landlord throw his cards down on the table and rush over to the bed. He was red in the face and yelled, 'You old swine! Spitting the children in the eye, are you!'

'But good grief, man, they wouldn't leave him alone!' I shouted, beside myself. However, being fearful all along that I might get thrown out, I didn't put much force into my shout; only, my whole body trembled with rage.

The landlord turned around toward me.

'Ho, listen to that! What the hell does it have to do with you? You just keep your mouth shut and do as I say, that's your best bet.'

But now the matron's voice could also be heard, and the whole house resounded with wrangling.

'I believe, God help me, you must be stark-staring mad, all of you!' she screamed. 'If you want to stay in here you'll have to keep quiet, both of you, take it from me! Huh, it isn't enough that one has to fix the poor devil up with room and board, one must put up with doomsday and commotion and devilish nuisance in one's own house as well. But that will have to stop, take it from me! Ssh. Shut your traps, kids, and wipe your noses, too, or I'll come and do it for you! I've never seen the likes of such people! Here they come in straight from the street, without even a penny to buy lice ointment, kick up a row in the middle of the night and make mischief among the people who

live here. I want none of it, understand, and all those of
you who don't belong here can make yourselves scarce. I
want peace in my own house, I tell you!'

I said not a word, didn't even open my mouth, but sat
down near the door again and listened to the uproar.
Everyone joined in the clamour, even the children and the
maid, who tried to explain how the quarrel had started.
If I just kept quiet, it would probably blow over sooner
or later; it would surely not come to the worst as long as
I didn't say anything. What could I say anyway? Wasn't
it winter outside, and wasn't night coming on, to boot?
Was this the time to pound the table and show you could
hold your own? No tomfooleries, please! And so I sat still
and didn't leave the house, though I had very nearly been
given notice. Hardened, I stared at the wall, where Christ
was hanging in an oleograph, and kept stubbornly silent
amid all the landlady's sallies.

'Well, if it's me you want to get rid of, ma'am, nothing
stands in the way as far as I am concerned,' one of the
card players said.

He stood up. The other card player stood up too.

'No, I didn't mean you. Not you either,' the landlady
answered the two of them. 'If necessary, I'll show whom
I mean, all right. If necessary. Take it from me. We shall
see who it is.'

She spoke in spurts and gave me these jabs at short
intervals, dragging it out to let me know more clearly
that it was me she had in mind. Quiet! I said to myself.
Just quiet! She hadn't asked me to leave, not expressly,
not in so many words. Only, no arrogance on my part, no
misplaced pride! Keep all your wits about you! . . . How

curiously green the hair of that Christ in the oleograph was. It had a distinct resemblance to green grass or, expressed with studied precision: thick meadow grass. Ha, a perfectly correct remark on my part, reasonably thick meadow grass. . . . A succession of fleeting associations of ideas flashed through my head at this moment – from the green grass to a Bible passage that says all flesh is as grass that is torched, and from there to Judgment Day when everything would be burned up, then a small detour to the Lisbon earthquake, whereupon I had a dim memory of a Spanish brass spittoon and an ebony penholder I had seen at Ylajali's. Alas, all was perishable! Just like grass that was torched. It all came to four boards and a shroud – at Madam Andersen's, main entrance to the right. . . .

All this was tossed around in my head in this desperate moment when my landlady was about to throw me out of the house.

'He doesn't hear!' she cried. 'I'm telling you to leave this house, now you know! Strike me dead, I believe the man must be insane! Now, get out, this blessed minute, and no more idle talk.'

I looked towards the door, not to leave, not at all to leave – an audacious idea occurred to me: if there had been a key in the door I would have turned it, locking myself in with the others to avoid leaving. I felt an absolutely hysterical horror at the thought of ending up on the street again. But there wasn't any key in the door and I got up; there was no hope left.

Then my landlord's voice suddenly mingles with his wife's. Astonished, I remained standing. The same man who had recently threatened me takes my side, strangely enough. He says, 'You can't throw people out on the street at night, you know. You can go to jail for that.'

I didn't know if you could go to jail for it, I didn't think so, but perhaps it was true, and the wife soon thought better of it, calmed down and didn't say another word to me. She even put out two sandwiches for my supper, but I didn't accept them – I didn't accept them solely because of my gratitude to the husband, pretending that I had eaten in town.

When I finally went out into the hall to go to bed, the matron followed me, stopped on the threshold and said loudly, her big pregnant belly bulging out toward me, 'But this is the last night you're sleeping here, now you know.'

'All right,' I answered.

By tomorrow something might turn up in the way of shelter if I put real effort into it. I was bound to find some sort of hiding place. For the time being I was glad not to have to spend the night in the open.

I slept until five or six in the morning. It wasn't light yet when I awoke, but I got up right away all the same. I had slept fully clothed because of the cold, so there was nothing more to put on. After drinking some water and quietly opening the door, I went out at once, as I was afraid of meeting my landlady again.

The only living things I saw in the street were a few policemen who had been on patrol all night. Shortly afterwards some men began to put out the street lamps all around. I drifted about aimlessly, got up to Kirke Street and headed down toward the Fortress. Cold and still sleepy, my knees and back tired from my long walk, and very hungry, I sat down on a bench and fell into a long doze. For three weeks I had been living exclusively on the sandwiches my landlady had given me morning and evening. It was now exactly twenty-four hours since I had had my last meal, my hunger pains were becoming severe once more, and I had to find a way out fairly soon. With this thought, I fell asleep again on the bench. . . .

I was awakened by people talking nearby, and when I had gathered my wits about me I saw it was broad daylight and that everyone was up and about. I stood up and walked off. The sun was bursting forth over the hills, the sky was nice and clear, and in my joy at the beautiful morning after so many dark weeks I forgot all my worries and thought I had been worse off many a time. I slapped my chest and sang a snatch of song to myself. My voice sounded so poor, downright feeble, I was moved to tears by it. Also, this gorgeous day, that clear sky flooded with light, affected me all too deeply, and I burst into loud sobs.

'What's the matter with you?' some man asked.

I didn't answer, just hurried off, hiding my face from everybody.

I came down to the docks. A big barque with a Russian flag was unloading coal; I read its name, *Copégoro*, on the ship's side. I found it amusing for a while to observe what was going on aboard the foreign ship. It must have been almost completely unloaded, sitting already with IX feet naked on the stem despite the ballast it had taken in by now, and when the coal-heavers trampled along the deck in their heavy boots, the entire ship gave a hollow boom.

The sun, the light, the salty breath from the ocean, all this lively, bustling activity stiffened my backbone and set my heart throbbing. All at once it occurred to me that I might do a couple of scenes of my play while sitting here. I took my sheets of paper from my pocket.

I tried to shape up some lines from the lips of a monk, lines that ought to swell with intolerance and power, but I didn't succeed. So I skipped the monk and tried to work out a speech, that which the judge addressed to the desecrator of the temple, and I wrote half a page of this speech, whereupon I stopped. My words just wouldn't evoke the right atmosphere. The bustling activity around me, the sea shanties, the noise of the capstans, and the incessant clanking of the railway-carriage couplings agreed poorly with that thick, musty air of mediaevalism which was to envelop my play, like fog. I gathered up my papers and got up.

Still, I had made a wonderful start, and I was confident I could now accomplish something if all went well. If only I had someplace to go! I thought hard – I actually stopped in the middle of the street to think – but didn't come up with a single quiet place in the whole city where I could settle down for a while. I had no choice but to go back to the rooming house in the Vaterland section. Though I shrank from the very thought of this, telling myself all along it just wouldn't do, I inched forward all the same and came closer and closer to the forbidden spot. It was cowardly, to be sure, that I admitted to myself – it was, in fact, disgraceful, downright disgraceful; but there was no help for it. I wasn't the least bit proud. I dare say I was one of the least cocky creatures in existence these days. And so I went.

I stopped at the entrance and pondered the matter yet once more. Yes, I had to risk it, come what may. The whole thing was a mere nothing anyway. First, it would only be for a few hours; second, God forbid I should ever take refuge in that house again, at some later date! I went into the courtyard. Picking my way over the uneven cobbles in the yard, I still felt uncertain and very nearly turned around at the door. I clenched my teeth. No, none of your misplaced pride now! If worst came to worst, I could always give the excuse that I had dropped in to say goodbye, take proper leave, and to come to an agreement concerning my small debt to the house. I opened the door to the hall.

Once inside, I remained stock-still. Right in front of me, two steps away, stood the landlord himself, without hat and coat, peeping through the keyhole into the family room. He made mute gestures with his hand to make me stay quiet and peeped through the keyhole again. He was laughing.

'Come over here,' he said in a whisper.

I approached on tiptoe.

'Just look!' he said, laughing with quiet, excited laughter. 'Take a peep! Hee-hee! There they lie. Look at the old man! Can you see the old man?'

In the bed, right below Christ's oleograph and directly opposite me, I could see two figures, the landlady and the strange mate; her legs gleamed white against the dark quilt. And on the bed by the other wall sat her father, the paralysed greybeard, looking on, hunched over his hands and curled up as usual, without being able to move.

I turned around to my landlord. He had the greatest difficulty keeping from laughing aloud. He was holding his hand over his nose.

'Did you see the old man?' he whispered. 'Oh Lord, did you see the old man? The way he sits there looking on!' He put his face to the keyhole again.

I went over to the window and sat down. This spectacle had thrown all my thoughts into merciless confusion and upset my rich mood. Why, what was it to me? When the husband himself put up with it, was even greatly amused by it, there was no reason why I should take it to heart. And as far as the old man was concerned, the old man was an old man. Maybe he didn't even see it, maybe he just sat there sleeping; God knows, he might even be dead. It wouldn't surprise me if he was dead sitting there. I felt no qualms about it.

I picked up my papers again and tried to dismiss all extraneous impressions. I had stopped in the middle of a sentence of the judge's speech: And so God and the law bid me, the counsel of my wise men bids me, and so too my own conscience bids me . . . I looked out the window to consider what his conscience should bid him do. A small noise reached my ears from the living room. Oh, it was no concern of mine, not in the least; besides, the old greybeard was dead – he could have died this morning, around four. Consequently, I didn't care two hoots about that noise. Why the hell, then, was I sitting there troubling my head about it? Quiet now!

And so too my own conscience bids me . . .

But everything conspired against me. The husband didn't keep altogether quiet over by the keyhole, not by any means, I could hear his suppressed laughter every now and then and saw him shaking. Out in the street there was also something going on that distracted me. A small boy was pottering by himself in the sun on the far pavement; completely off his guard, he sat there tying together some strips of paper and wasn't bothering anybody. Suddenly he jumps up and curses. Backing into the street, he catches sight of a man, a grown man with a red beard, who was leaning out of an open second-floor window and spitting down on his head. The little fellow cried from anger and cursed helplessly up at the window, and the man just laughed in his face. Five minutes may have gone by that way. I turned away to avoid seeing the boy's tears.

And so too my own conscience bids me . . .

I found it impossible to get any further. In the end my mind seemed to be giving way, and I came to think that even what I had already written was unusable; indeed, that the whole idea was awful nonsense. One couldn't really talk about conscience in the Middle Ages, the conscience was only invented by Shakespeare, that old dancing master, and consequently my whole speech was wrong. So was there nothing of value in these pages? I leafed through them afresh and dispelled my doubts immediately; I found some magnificent parts, quite long passages that were really extraordinary. An intoxicating urge to set to work again and finish my play swept through me once more.

I got up and went over to the door without heeding the

landlord's furious signs to me to step lightly. I walked firmly and resolutely out of the hall, up the stairs to the second floor, and entered my old room. The mate wasn't there, after all, so what stood in the way of my sitting here a moment? I wouldn't touch any of his things, wouldn't even use his table, but just settle on a chair near the door and be glad at that. I eagerly unfold the papers on my knees.

Now it went extremely well for several minutes. One speech after another sprang up in my head, perfectly finished, and I wrote without a break. I fill one page after another, tear along at full speed, murmuring softly with delight at my fine mood and scarcely knowing what I'm doing. The only sound I hear at this moment is my own joyful murmur. I also had a felicitous idea about a church bell that would burst out ringing at a certain point in my play. Everything was going sweepingly.

Then I hear footsteps on the stairs. I tremble, almost beside myself and ready to jump up at any moment, wary, alert, fearful of everything, and inflamed by hunger. I listen nervously, hold the pencil still in my hand and listen, unable to write another word. The door opens and the pair from the living room step in.

Even before I had time to apologise, the landlady shouted, thunderstruck, 'Goodness gracious, there he is again!'

'I beg your pardon!' I said. I would have said more but didn't get any further.

The landlady threw the door open all the way and screamed, 'I swear to God, if you don't leave this minute I'll call the police!'

I stood up.

'I just wanted to say goodbye,' I mumbled, 'and so I had to wait for you. I haven't touched a thing, I was just sitting here on this chair—'

'No harm done,' the mate said. 'Why the damn fuss? Just leave the man alone!'

Going down the stairs, I suddenly flew into a rage with this fat, bloated woman who was following hard on my heels to get rid of me in a hurry, and I stood still for a moment, my mouth full of the most awful epithets which I had a mind to spit at her. But I thought better of it and held my tongue – held my tongue out of gratitude to the stranger who walked behind her and would hear it all. The landlady was constantly pursuing me, hurling abuse without let-up, while my anger increased with every step that I took.

We came down into the yard, with me walking very slowly, still trying to decide whether to take on the landlady. I was at this moment frantic with rage, contemplating the most awful bloodshed, a blow that would strike her dead instantly, a kick in the belly. A messenger passes me in the entrance, he says hello but I don't answer. He turns to the matron behind me, and I can hear him asking for me. But I don't turn around.

A few steps outside the entrance the messenger catches up with me, says hello once more and stops me. He hands me a letter. Angry and reluctant, I tear it open – a ten-krone note falls out of the envelope, but no letter, not a word.

I look at the man and ask, 'What sort of silly prank is this? Who is this letter from?'

'I don't know,' he answers, 'but it was a lady who gave it to me.'

I stood still. The messenger left. I put the note back in the envelope, crumple it all up, turn around and walk up to the landlady, who is still keeping an eye on me from the entrance, and throw the note in her face. I didn't say anything, didn't utter a syllable, only noticed that she examined the crumpled-up paper before I left.

Ha, that's what was called knowing how to acquit oneself! Not say a word, not speak to the scum, but quite calmly crumple up a big note and throw it straight in the face of one's persecutors. That's what one could call behaving with dignity. It served them right, the brutes!

When I got to the corner of Tomte Street and Jærnbanetorvet Square, the street suddenly began swirling before my eyes, there was an empty buzzing in my head, and I fell up against the wall of a building. I simply couldn't walk any further, couldn't even straighten up from my awkward position. I remained slumped over against the wall, just as I had fallen, and I felt I was about to pass out. My insane anger was only heightened by this fit of exhaustion, and I lifted my foot and stamped it on the pavement. I also did various other things to recover my strength: I clenched my teeth, knitted my brows and rolled my eyes in despair, and it began to help. My mind cleared up, I understood I was about to go under. I stretched out my hands and pushed myself back from the wall; the street was still whirling around with me. Bursting into sobs of rage, I fought my distress with my innermost soul, bravely holding my own so as not to fall down: I had no intention of collapsing, I would die on my feet. A cart rolled slowly

by. I see there are potatoes in the cart, but out of rage,
from sheer obstinacy, I take it into my head to say they
weren't potatoes at all, they were cabbages, and I swore
horribly that they were cabbages. I heard quite well what
I said, and I swore wilfully time after time, upholding
this lie just to have the droll satisfaction of committing
downright perjury. Drunk with this unprecedented sin, I
raised three fingers and swore with quivering lips in the
name of the Father, the Son, and the Holy Ghost that they
were cabbages.

Time passed. I let myself sink down on the steps nearby
and wiped the sweat off my forehead and my neck, took
a deep breath and forced myself to be calm. The sun was
going down, the afternoon was wearing on. I began once
more to brood on my situation. My hunger was getting
outrageous, and in a few hours it would be night again;
I had to think of a way out while there was still time. My
thoughts began again to circle around the rooming house
I had been driven away from; I certainly didn't want to
go back there but still couldn't help thinking about it.
Actually, the woman had every right in the world to
throw me out. How could I expect people to put me
up if I didn't pay them! What's more, she had given me
food off and on; even last night, after I had provoked her,
she had offered me two sandwiches, offered them to me
out of kindness because she knew that I needed them. So
I had nothing to complain about, and as I sat there on
the steps I began to ask – no, beg – her forgiveness in
my heart for the way I had behaved. Most of all, I was
bitterly sorry I had shown myself ungrateful to her at the
end and thrown that piece of paper in her face. . . .

The ten-krone note! I gave a whistle. The letter the messenger brought, where did it come from? Only now, at this moment, did I think clearly about this, and I had a hunch right away what the story was. Sick with pain and shame, I whispered 'Ylajali' several times in a hoarse voice and shook my head. Was it not me who had decided only yesterday to walk proudly past her when we met and to display the utmost indifference toward her? And instead of that I had merely aroused her compassion and coaxed her out of a pennyworth of charity. No, no, no, there was no end to my degradation! Not even vis-à-vis her had I been able to maintain a respectable posture; I was sinking, sinking everywhere I turned, sinking to my knees, to my middle, going down in infamy never to come up again, never! That beat everything! To accept ten kroner of alms money without being able to throw it back at the secret donor, to scramble for pennies with both hands wherever they were offered, hang onto them, use them to pay the rent despite my own innermost repugnance. . . .

Couldn't I put my hands on those ten kroner again somehow or other? Going back to the landlady to get the note returned wouldn't do any good, of course; but there must be some other way if I stopped to think, if I just tried really hard to stop and think about it. Here, honest to God, it wasn't sufficient to think just in the ordinary way, I had to think about some means of procuring those ten kroner till my whole body ached. I sat down to think hard.

It was probably around four by now, in a couple of hours I might get to see the theatre manager if my play had been finished. I take out the manuscript on the spot

and try to put together the three or four last scenes, by
hook or by crook. I think and sweat and read it through
from the beginning but can't get anywhere. No nonsense,
now! I say, no bullheadedness there! And so I work
for dear life on my play, writing down everything that
comes to mind just to finish quickly and be off. I tried to
convince myself I was having another big moment, lying
to my face and openly deceiving myself while scribbling
away as though there was no need to look for the right
words. That's good! That's a real find! I whispered every
so often, just get it down! Eventually, however, my most
recent lines of dialogue began to sound suspicious to me:
they contrasted so sharply with the dialogue in the early
scenes. Besides, there wasn't the slightest tinge of the
Middle Ages about the monk's words. I break my pencil
between my teeth, jump up, tear my manuscript to bits,
every single sheet, toss my hat in the gutter and trample
it. 'I'm lost!' I whisper to myself. 'Ladies and gentlemen,
I'm lost!' I say nothing except these words as I stand there
trampling my hat.

A few steps away a policeman is observing me; he
stands in the middle of the street and doesn't pay attention
to anything else. Our eyes meet as I lift my head; maybe he
had been standing there for quite a while just watching
me. I pick up my hat, put it on, and walk over to
the man.

'Do you know what time it is?' I ask.

He waits a while before pulling out his watch, not
taking his eyes off me for a moment.

'A little past four,' he says.

'Exactly!' I say. 'A little past four, perfectly correct!

You know your stuff, I see, and I'll be thinking about you.'

With that I left him. I threw him into a state of the utmost astonishment, and he followed me with his eyes, mouth agape, still holding the watch in his hand. When I had reached the Royal Hotel I turned around and looked back; he was still standing in the same position, following me with his eyes.

Hee-hee, that's the way to treat those brutes! With the most refined impudence! That impressed the brutes, gave them a fright. . . . I was extremely pleased with myself and began again to sing a snatch of song. Tense with excitement, feeling no pain any more, or even any kind of discomfort, I walked through the whole market light as a feather, turned around at the Arcades and settled on a bench near Our Saviour's.

Might it not, after all, be a matter of indifference whether I returned a ten-krone note or not? Once I had received it, it was mine, and there certainly wasn't any want where it came from. Anyway, I couldn't help accepting it, since it was sent expressly to me; it wouldn't have made any sense to let the messenger keep it. Nor would it do to return an entirely different ten-krone note than the one I had received. So, there was nothing to be done about it.

I tried to look at the traffic around the market in front of me and occupied my thoughts with indifferent things; but I didn't succeed and was still taken up with the ten-krone note. Finally I clenched my hands and got angry. She would feel hurt, I said, if I sent it back, so why should I do it? I was always ready to consider myself too good for this, that and the other, to shake my head arrogantly and say, No, thanks! Now I could see what it led to: I found myself once more on the street. Even when I had the best opportunity to do so, I didn't hold onto my nice, warm lodging; I turned proud, jumped up at the first word and brazened it out, handed out ten kroner left and right and went my way. . . . I took myself sharply to task for having abandoned my lodging and once again landing myself in a quandary.

For the rest, I didn't give a tinker's damn about the whole business. I hadn't asked for that ten-krone note and had barely held it in my hands, I had given it away at once, paid it out to some total strangers I would never see again. That was the sort of man I was, always paying down to the last mite when something was at stake. If I knew Ylajali rightly, she wasn't sorry she had sent me that money either, so what was I carrying on for? Actually, it was the least she could do to send me a ten-krone note every now and then. After all, the poor girl was in love with me, ha! perhaps even hopelessly in love with me. . . . And I sat there puffing myself up at this thought. There could be no doubt that she was in love with me, the poor girl! . . .

It turned five o'clock. After my long bout of nervous excitement, I collapsed anew and began once more to hear that empty buzzing in my head. My eyes fixed in a blank stare, I looked in the direction of the Elephant Pharmacy. Hunger was raging fiercely inside me and I was in great pain. As I sit thus looking into vacancy, a figure is gradually revealed to my fixed stare, one that I finally see quite distinctly and recognise: it is the cake vendor by the Elephant Pharmacy.

I give a start, draw myself up on the bench, and start thinking. Yes, sure enough, it was the same woman in front of the same table in the same spot! I whistle a couple of times and snap my fingers, get up from the bench and start walking toward the pharmacy. No nonsense now! I didn't give a damn whether it was the wages of sin or good Norwegian huckster's money minted in silver at Kongsberg! I wasn't going to be ridiculous, you could die from too much pride.

I walk over to the corner, aim for the woman and take my stand in front of her. I smile, nod familiarly, and frame my words as if it were a matter of course that I would be back someday.

'Hello!' I say. 'Perhaps you don't recognise me?'

'No,' she answers slowly, looking at me.

I smile even more broadly, as if it were only her funny little joke that she didn't know me, and say, 'Don't you remember that I gave you a stack of kroner one day? I didn't say anything on that occasion as far as I remember, that's true, I didn't; I don't usually do that. When you are dealing with honest people, it is unnecessary to make an agreement and, so to speak, sign a contract for every little thing. Hee-hee. Oh yes, it was I who handed over that money to you.'

'Really, so it was you! Yes, now I suppose I know you too, when I think back a little.'

Wanting to forestall her thanking me for the money, I say quickly, letting my eyes wander around her table in search of eatables, 'Well, here I've come to pick up the cakes.'

She doesn't understand.

'The cakes,' I repeat, 'I've come to pick them up. Some anyway, the first helping. I won't need them all today.'

'You've come to pick them up?' she asks.

'Yes, I've come to pick them up, most certainly I have!' I answer, laughing aloud, as though it ought to have been quite obvious to her from the very beginning that I had come to pick them up. And I grab a cake from the table, a kind of French roll, which I begin to eat.

When the woman sees this, she rises in her cellar hole and makes an instinctive gesture to protect her merchandise, giving me to understand that she hadn't expected me to be back to rob her of it.

'You hadn't?' I say. 'Indeed, you hadn't?' What a funny woman she was! Had it ever happened to her that someone gave her a chunk of kroner for safekeeping without that person asking to get it back? No! Well, there you are! Maybe she thought it was stolen money, since I had tossed it to her like that? Ah, she didn't! That was nice anyway, very nice. It was, if I might say so, sweet of her to take me for an honest man at least. Haw-haw! Oh, she was a good one, all right!

But why, then, did I give her the money? The woman got furious and raised a hue and cry.

I explained why I had given her the money, explained it quietly and emphatically: I was in the habit of acting like that because I had such faith in everybody. Whenever someone offered me a contract or an IOU, I always shook my head and said, No, thanks! As God was my witness, I did.

But the woman still didn't understand.

I tried another tack, spoke sharply and refused to listen

to any nonsense. Hadn't it ever happened to her to be paid in advance in the same way? I asked. Of course, I meant by people who were well off, some of the consuls, for example? Never? Well, it wasn't fair that I should suffer because she was unfamiliar with this social custom. It was accepted practice in foreign countries. But maybe she had never been abroad? Ah, there you are! Then she didn't have a word to say in this matter. . . . And I made a grab for several cakes on the table.

She gave an angry growl, doggedly refusing to hand over anything from her table, she even snatched a piece of cake out of my hand and put it back in its place. I got very angry, banged the table and threatened her with the police. I would be easy on her, I said; if I took everything that belonged to me, her entire business would be ruined, because it was an awful lot of money I had given her that time. But I wouldn't take that much – in fact, I was asking only for half my money's worth. And as an extra I promised never to be back again. God forbid, seeing that she was that sort of person.

Finally she put out some cakes, at an outrageous price, four or five pieces which she appraised at the highest rate she could think of, told me to take them and clear off. I still bickered with her, insisting that she was cheating me out of at least one krone of the money and, what's more, was bleeding me white with her gouging prices. 'Don't you know you can go to jail for such dirty tricks?' I said. 'May God help you. You could get hard labour for life, you old fool!' She threw me yet another cake and, all but grinding her teeth, told me to be gone.

I left.

Huh, who ever saw such a dishonest cake vendor! As I walked through the marketplace munching my cakes, I talked aloud without stopping about the woman and her insolence, repeating to myself what we had said to each other and thinking I'd had a big edge over her. I ate the cakes in front of everybody, talking about this.

The cakes disappeared one after another, but however much I put away it didn't help, my hunger was just as bottomless. Good God, why didn't it help? I was so greedy that I nearly laid hands on the last cake, which I had decided at the very outset to save for that little fellow down in Vognmand Street, the boy who had been spat at on the head by the man with the red beard. I kept thinking about him all the time – I couldn't make myself forget his expression as he leaped up, crying and cursing. He had turned around to my window when the man spat at him, and he had plainly checked whether I, too, would laugh at him. God only knew if I would find him when I got down there! I went all out to get to Vognmand Street in a hurry, passed the spot where I had torn up my play and where some bits of paper were still floating around, evaded the police officer whom I had so astonished by my behaviour recently, and stood at last at the steps where the boy had been sitting.

He wasn't there. The street was almost empty. It was beginning to get dark and I couldn't spot the boy; maybe he had gone in. I put the cake down carefully, leaning it up against the door, knocked hard and ran off at once. He is sure to find it! I said to myself. He'll find it first thing when he comes out! And my eyes grew moist with foolish glee at the thought that the little fellow would find the cake.

I came down to the Jærnbane Pier again.

I wasn't hungry any more, but the sweet food I had eaten was beginning to make me sick. My head was again awhirl with the wildest fancies: What if I secretly cut the hawser of one of those ships? What if I suddenly started yelling fire? I walk further out on the pier, find myself a crate to sit on and fold my hands, feeling my head getting more and more confused. I am quite motionless, not lifting a finger to tough it out any longer.

I sit there staring at *Copégoro*, the barque with the Russian flag. I make out a man at the rail; the red lantern on the port side shines down on his head, and I stand up and call out to him. I didn't have any purpose in acting as I did, nor did I expect to get an answer. I said, 'Do you sail tonight, Captain?'

'Yes, in a little while,' the man answers. He spoke Swedish. Then he was probably a Finn, I thought.

'Hmm. You aren't a man short, are you?' I didn't care at that moment whether I was refused or not, it was all the same to me what answer the man would give me. I waited, looking at him.

'Well, no,' he said. 'It would be a deck hand, in any case.'

A deck hand! I gave myself a shake, slipped my glasses off on the sly and put them in my pocket, stepped onto the gangway and strode on board.

'I'm not an able seaman,' I said, 'but I can do whatever you bid me to. Where are you bound for?'

'We sail with ballast to Leeds, to take in coal for Cádiz.'

'Fine!' I said, forcing myself on the man. 'It's all one to me where we're going. I'll do my job.'

He stood a while eyeing me, thinking it over.

'You haven't gone to sea before, have you?' he asked.

'No. But as I'm telling you, give me a job and I'll do it. I'm used to a little of everything.'

He thought it over again. I had already set my mind on going along, and I began to fear getting chased ashore again.

'So what do you say, Captain?' I asked at last. 'I can really do anything, whatever you wish. What am I saying? I would have to be a poor fellow if I didn't do more than just what I was set to do. I can take two watches in a row if necessary. It'll do me a world of good, and I believe I can take it.'

'All right, we can give it a try,' he said, smiling faintly at my last words. 'If it doesn't work out, we can always part company in England.'

'Of course!' I answered, overjoyed. And I repeated that we could part company in England if it didn't work out.

Then he put me to work.

Once out in the fjord I straightened up, wet with fever and fatigue, looked in towards the shore and said goodbye for now to the city, to Kristiania, where the windows shone so brightly in every home.

Translator's Trap:
Knut Hamsun's *Hunger* in English

SVERRE LYNGSTAD

If the narrator of Knut Hamsun's *Hunger* could have foreseen the abuse his story would suffer at the hands of translators, his demonic rebellion would surely have been considerably heightened. Both the English rendering of 1899 by George Egerton, alias of Mary Chavelita Dunne,[1] and Robert Bly's American one of 1967[2] have egregious flaws that might cause any author to despair of ever being understood beyond the confines of his or her own national culture.

In terms of general correctness, the English translation is by far the better one. Though there are some mistranslations, they are few by comparison with those in the American version. Strangely enough, this does not mean that Ms Dunne's rendering is faithful to the original, since she felt compelled to expurgate the text of all explicitly erotic content. The most she allowed to slip through the Victorian censor that must have been operating at the back of her mind was a kiss or an embrace. Consequently, large segments of Parts Three and Four, specifically those presenting the story of the narrator's abortive rendezvous with Ylajali (Part Three) and his voyeuristic description of the sexual encounter between his landlady and the young lodger (Part Four), were eliminated. With these mutilations, her version cannot be said to be a rendering of Hamsun's novel at all.

While the American edition avoids bowdlerisation, it is no more faithful to Hamsun's text. Nor is the book particularly readable. The reasons for this judgment will emerge from the following discussion.

Hunger poses a great challenge to the translator. Hamsun's vocabulary is extensive, and he exploits it with subtlety and a fine sense of nuance. The range of expressiveness of his language is vastly extended by folksy idiom, standard or frozen expressions that have no direct, easily discovered equivalents in any other language. Add to these features the stylistic complexities that arise from the novel's intense psychological focus, with its near-inevitable demand for figurative language, and we realise just how formidable a task the translator is confronted with in trying to produce a faithful as well as readable text in English.

It looks as though the American translator was either unaware of these difficulties or decided to produce his own text, using Hamsun's original as a mere pretext for undertaking an independent creation. It is hard to tell whether the inaccuracies and errors are due to insufficient knowledge of the source language, or to a slapdash, pseudo-creative attitude toward the craft of translation. Whatever the reasons, the sheer number of wrong or merely half- or quarter-right renderings of words and phrases is overwhelmingly high, easily running to four digits. That is to say, there are on average five such mistaken renderings per page. Some are what I would consider real howlers, stemming from a radical misreading of a word, phrase or clause.

I have classified these mistakes into seven categories, with fleeting boundaries. The order used in presenting the individual examples is as follows: the Norwegian word or phrase, the translation used in the American edition, a reasonably correct translation.

1. *Misreading of idiomatic expressions*: vildt fremmed Menneske (13)[3] / heathen savage (10) / total stranger (9) / / hun var syndig søt (27) / that sort of magnificence ought to have been prohibited (28–29) / she was ravishingly sweet (23) / / gjøre ærlig Rede for mig (31) / make some honest nest for myself (34) / explain myself in all honesty (27) / / Hvad mon det led på Dagen (35) / What would this day bring? (39) / How late in the day was it? I wondered (31) / / Det er Fan heller! (43) / It's not, more likely the devil! (49) / Like hell it is! (40) / / han har for Vane å støte litt i Næsen nu og da (96) / one of his quirks was brushing his nose with his thumb every once in a while (119) / he has a habit of snorting slightly every once in a while (97) / / Å hør, med det samme jeg husker det (133) / Never mind, suddenly I remember it (165) / Listen, come to think of it (134) / / Det er sandt! (154) / The truth is the truth (191) / By the way, or Come to think of it (156) / / komme til Kræfter (178) / come to (221) / recover my strength (180) / / Syndens Penger (182) / coins . . . from the devil's private stock (227) / the wages of sin (185).

2. *Literal* or *quasi-literal rendering of metaphorical expressions*: Men det skal De være blå for (116) / Well, you'll have to turn blue in the face from waiting then (143) / But you won't get your way (116) / / Jeg gav hende en god Dag (164) / I said goodbye to her (204) / I didn't give a hang about her (167).

3. *Construing words etymologically*: Der skulde jeg altså havne! (86) / That was where my ship would tie up! (105) / So that was where I would end up! (85) / / Jungmand (186) / young man (231) / deck hand, ordinary seaman (189).

4. *Misreading of tone*: det var bare en liten Knipe jeg stod i (50) / I wasn't in a really big fix anyway (58) / I just happen to be in a tight spot (47) / / Kjære, snille Dem! (143) / My sweet thing! (179) / Please, please! (145) [Ylajali begging the hero to stop trying to force her sexually] / / Jo, hun var virkelig god! (183) / She was really a very good person! (228) / She was a good one, all right! (186)

5. *Misreading of near homophones and of words with multiple meanings*: Lærhalsbånd (107) / training collar (132) / leather collar (107) / / Så byder mig og min egen Samvittighet (175) / My self and my own conscience tell me to do this; therefore (217) / So too my own conscience bids me ('og' taken to mean 'and' instead of 'also' or 'too') (177) / / hikste av Raseri (178) / hiccup from fury (221) / sobs of rage (181) / / trak Veiret til mig (178) / fanned myself (222) / took a deep breath (181).

6. *Grammatical misconception*: Det farer som en Strøm av Lys gjennem mit bryst (52) / The letter shot through me like a stream of light (61) / A stream of light seems to surge through my breast (49) / / gik og sprang om hverandre (39) / walked and ran around everyone (44) / walked and ran by turns (35) / / nede i Tværgaten (103) / down in Tvær Street (127) / in the side street (103).

7. *Choosing word meanings mistakenly or arbitrarily*: Så jeg kunde aldeles ikke begripe mig på det hele (60) / So I had nothing at all to rebuke myself with on that score (72) / So I couldn't make head nor tail of the whole situation (58) / / med . . . Hænderne hæftet i mit Frakkefald (69) / with my hands clasped beneath my coattails (83) / with . . . my hands gripping my lapels (67) / / sultet mig Forstanden ut av Hjærnen (85) / starved my hairs out of my head (104) / starved till my wits took leave of my brain (84) / / Damelæger (86) / lady-killer (105) / women's physicians (85) / / Da måtte jeg være grøn! (143) / I must be firm, then! (178) / How naive could I be! (145) / / Jeg var vel bevaret (157) / I was in good shape (196) / I was in my right mind (160) / / Jo det hadde sin Rigtighet (182) / All this had its own justice (226) / Yes, sure enough (185).

These are only a handful of examples; there are hundreds of almost equally egregious errors in the translation.

The cumulative effect of such errors, when combined with numerous additions, omissions (particularly of those small words, modifiers and transitional expressions that help to establish the tone of a sentence), excessive licence in construing the text, simplifications (especially of words denoting psychological states), hyperbole and a tendency toward colloquialisms and slang, is to produce a mockery of the original. In the following I shall discuss a few specific features of the translator's practice to show how they falsify Hamsun's text.

Hunger is an urban novel, whose action takes place within a distinctive setting of streets, squares and residential areas familiar to Kristiania (now Oslo) residents. A translation ought to reproduce this geography as clearly as possible, first, as a matter of principle; second, to help the reader get oriented to the urban setting; third, to permit Hamsun aficionados to emulate those Joyceans who have been faithfully retracing the Dublin itinerary of Leopold Bloom on that famous June day in 1904.

However, in this instance the sentimental traveller or literary pilgrim would be hard pressed to relate the map of the city of Oslo to the implicit geography of the American text. For one thing, entire neighbourhoods have been converted into streets, such as Grønland, Hammersborg, Hægdehaugen and Vaterland, all of which are residential sections. Youngstorvet is a square, not a street, whereas Grønlandsleret is the name of a street; confusion results from translating the latter as Grønland Street. Studenterlunden, a park-like promenade near the university, is sometimes called just 'Lunden' by Hamsun. The translator's handling of this name ranges from the 'Students' Promenade' to simply 'trees' (p. 15). The Palace Park (Slotsparken) is variously rendered as the 'public gardens' and the 'Royal Gardens', and Slotsbakken (Palace Hill) is treated as a common noun ('hill', p. 13).

Norway did not then, and does not today, have a 'Senate House', since it lacks a senate. If one feels called upon to translate 'Storting', the proper term would be Parliament, or the Parliament Building. 'Logen' means the 'Lodge Building', not 'ticket office' (p. 45). The significance of the narrator's obsession with 'Stiftsgården', a structure that no longer exists, is that in the late 1880s when Hamsun's novel was written, this building was the residence of the Prime Minister. Whether it is taken to mean, mistakenly, 'expensive club' (p. 76) or 'Governor's Mansion' (p. 94), in either case the magnitude of the hero's bizarre whims is diminished. Finally, in Norway the floors of buildings are numbered as in the United States. The translation is in this respect inconsistent, alternating for some reason between the Continental and the American (and Norwegian) practice.

The temporal setting is also relevant to a translator's decisions on how to approach and reproduce a text. This does not mean that translation should be considered as a species of literary archaeology; such an approach would inevitably fail to produce a readable text. Nevertheless, it is important to recognise the stylistic character of the source text. In my view, Hamsun's narrative style in *Hunger* is on the whole conservative, at least in terms of diction, befitting the period. His syntax, on the other hand, is quite free. His extensive use of parataxis gives the narrative a somewhat abrupt, staccato rhythm. The translator must try to reproduce the evident tension resulting from these opposite tendencies.

This stylistic tension has a counterpart in the book's oscillating narrative point of view. As the first and the last sentence of the novel – both in the past tense – indicate, the story is told in retrospect. Though it may seem far-fetched to invoke the Wordsworthian definition of poetry as 'emotion recollected in tranquillity', it would be mistaken to deny altogether the relevance of such a definition to Hamsun's narrative voice in *Hunger*. There does exist a distance between the narrator and the experiencing hero. This is clear from Hamsun's use of the past tense alone. However, the distance often shrinks to such a degree that the retrospective narrator and the experiencing character appear to merge into one. Hamsun's frequent recourse to the present tense in the narrative proper signalises this near-merging. This alternation between the past and present tense in the narrative discourse of *Hunger* can be related to an Apollonian-Dionysian polarity that goes to the heart of Hamsun's aesthetic in this novel. However, neither of the two translations here discussed respected Hamsun's radical departure from conventional past-tense narrative, with the result that the alternation between near-identification and distancing in the narrator's posture has been lost. The present tense seems to have been automatically converted by both translators into the more usual past tense.

If the above hypothesis of a profound emotional tension in Hamsun's novel has any validity, a translator should avoid having recourse to any devices that would be conducive to reducing or eliminating it. It would, for example, be wrong to try to jazz up Hamsun's narrative by means of overly colloquial or slangy language or by an excessively loose, slapdash syntax. The American translation sins in both these respects, causing Hamsun's language to lose much of its range and contradictory complexity. Because of the periodic breakthrough of near-frenzy in the central character, there are moments when extreme usages are in order, to convey his emotional turbulence. The trouble is that if one adopts, as the translator seems to have done, an overly expressive or emphatic style, a style of hyperbole, the nuances are lost: Apollo is squelched by Dionysus. Would it not have been wiser to respect Hamsun's usage of the present tense and achieve some of the narrative intensification in that way?

Curiously enough, though, the translation seems to embody a tension, or contradiction, of its own, namely, between the above-mentioned tendency toward hyperbole in its various guises, on the one hand, and a surprisingly flat, unemphatic or abstract rendering of words and expressions on the other. The latter may be due to a limited knowledge of the nuances of certain Norwegian, or Dano-Norwegian, words. For a list of words and phrases that are 'hyperbolic' in relation to the source text, see Appendix, pp. 191–5.

A rather special instance of excessive expressiveness is the translator's handling of words of obviously metaphoric origin and of so-called stereotypic or frozen expressions, often clichés with a figurative base. (A few examples have been given under the heading of 'howlers'. For a generous sampling see Appendix, pp. 195–6.) Such phrases are usually idiomatic expressions, which means that they cannot be translated literally without producing verbosity, gaucherie or absurdity. Specifically, those that are dead metaphors should not be rendered in such a

way as to revive the metaphor, thereby creating an irrel-
evant and, most likely, disturbing intrusion of misplaced
concreteness. On the other hand, there is no reason why
one cannot try to find near-equivalents in the target
language, frozen expressions that have a comparable
force and flavour.

Reviving dead metaphors may be a fascinating device
for a poet who wishes to experiment with language;
even playwrights exploit them occasionally for parody
and ironic satire, as Edward Albee did in *The American
Dream*. But because such a strategy focuses the reader's
attention on the play of the signifier rather than on
what is signified, it does not work well in fiction where
language is primarily a medium for conveying action or a
succession of states of mind. The intrusive quality of such
a strategy becomes even more obvious where single words
are reduced to their etymological origin, such as 'havne'
and 'strande' in the American translation of *Hunger*. To
render 'havne' as 'tie up one's ship' and 'strande' as
'being left high and dry' instead of 'end up' and 'come
to grief' or 'fail', respectively, introduces an unintended
and disturbing distraction from the reality of the situation in either case. Bringing the buried word origins to
the surface by this kind of Heideggerian etymologising
is not a strategy to be recommended to translators of
fiction. Hamsun certainly did not play with language in
this way.

As I have already mentioned, the language of the
translation under review exhibits a polarity between two
tendencies: over-expressiveness and its opposite. The for-
mer appears not only as hyperbolic interpretations of

the word meanings of the original but also as exaggerated concreteness or specificity. Instances of excessive
concreteness will be found in the Appendix, pp. 197–8.

The opposite tendency is one that de-emphasises the
concrete and the sensory. There are numerous instances
where the American translation has suffered a loss of
concreteness or specificity vis-à-vis the original text. This
is particularly the case with words denoting acts of perception or psychological states. For example, 'fornemme'
(perceive), 'Fornemmelse' (perception, feeling), 'iagtta'
(observe) and 'Følelse' (sensation, feeling), all of which
refer to concrete sensory processes, are translated as 'recognise', 'conviction', 'examine' and 'conviction', respectively, words with much more abstract meanings denoting
an intellectual or moral act rather than a process of
observation or perception. As a result, the role of observer
that is so central to the main character in *Hunger*
veers toward that of a thinker. In some cases a general
or common word has replaced one with a more specific meaning. Thus, widely different Norwegian words
denoting nuances of mental or emotional distress – 'slapt'
(p. 123; limp), 'forsakt' (p. 142; crestfallen) and 'fortvilet'
(p. 158; desperate) – have all been translated by one and
the same English word: 'depressed' (pp. 152, 177, 197).
Other Norwegian words of similar meaning have been
rendered reductively by more common words in English,
like 'trouble', 'worry' and 'bother'. This produces an
effect of vagueness and imprecision that is absent from
Hamsun's text and distorts the book's tone. Again, the
word 'Gjenvordigheter' (adversity, tribulations, hard-
ship) has often a religious connotation when used in

Norwegian; 'setbacks' (p. 20) or 'trouble' (p. 123) are not appropriate renderings in English. Because of this flattening out of Hamsun's language the nuances of his psychological portraiture are greatly weakened, if not entirely lost. The jazzed-up diction elsewhere does not meet the problem. Specificity and subtlety cannot be compensated for by the kind of clamorous and often utterly meaningless linguistic noises that the translator has added to Hamsun's work. For a list of words and phrases illustrating reduced concreteness and specificity, see Appendix, pp. 198–201, which, while extensive, includes only a fraction of the relevant material.

The material cited provides ample evidence of contradictory principles of translation. Whether this is pure happenstance or the result of a deliberate decision, only the translator will know. At the beginning of my discussion I referred to other problems with the translation such as widespread omissions and additions, the latter amounting to veritable ad-libs. These alterations, whether a result of taking away from or adding to the text, of wrong connotations being produced or absurd statements turning up through failure to understand the text, do real violence to Hamsun's work. Here are a few more examples, exemplifying wordiness, wrong connotations and a seeming penchant for the bizarre, respectively.

The 'I' says that all his refusals from editors have made him 'forknyt' (p. 29), i.e. 'timid'; the American translator has: they 'had been a heavy blow to my morale' (p. 32). This is a not infrequent type of elaborate periphrasis in the book. Looking at the menu of a cheap restaurant, he 'trak opsigtsvækkende på Akslerne' (p. 43), i.e. 'he shrugged his shoulders conspicuously'. Instead we read: 'I . . . twitched my shoulders in case anyone was watching' (p. 50).

The most serious cases of wrong connotations pertain to Hamsun's allusions to the Bible, and to religious concepts in general. Reflecting on how God persecutes him, the hero 'looked up at the heavens' (så op mot det Høie, p. 21); to translate this by 'looked up to the sky' (p. 21) eliminates the religious connotation. A certain archaic flavour, along with echoes of the Biblical phrasing, is appropriate where the hero recalls the 'cadences of the Bible' (Bibelens Stiltone, p. 21). Inspired to write one morning, he asserts, 'og hvert Ord jeg skriver blir lagt mig i Munden' (p. 32). This is quite clearly a Biblical allusion. Instead of choosing Bly's formulation, 'and every word I set down came from somewhere else' (p. 36), one could render the phrase quite literally, in tune with Numbers 23:5: 'and every word I write is put in my mouth'. Preparing himself psychologically for meeting Pastor Levion, he refers, among other things, to 'det første fornødne' (p. 80), the 'one thing needful' (cf. Luke 10:42), curiously rendered by Bly as 'this is urgent' (p. 98), a phrase with not the least relish of Biblical prose. In the same passage the hero's disconsolate reflection that he doesn't even have 'spit in his lamp' (Spyt i Lampen, p. 80) sounds like an allusion to the foolish virgins with 'no oil' in their vessels (Matthew 25:3). The phrase 'not worth a tinker's damn' (p. 98), apart from the inappropriateness of a curse word in this context, reduces the element of Biblical parody in the passage. In another context of quasi-religious content, after the hero has relieved his conscience by giving away the money mistakenly returned to him by the store clerk, the phrase 'akslet mit Skind' (p. 120; girded up my loins) appears. While 'ready to do great deeds' (p. 148), the phrase used in the American translation, catches an essential part of the meaning, the Biblical allusion is again lost. Also, in the same passage, the phrase 'hemmelig Kummer' (p. 119) is not properly rendered as 'secret groan' (p. 148), which sounds crude, but as 'secret anguish', with its spiritual associations.

Conversely, it would seem wrong to convert more or less secular curses to religious ones, as happens with the mental exclamation, 'Det var da Satan til Menneske!' (p. 140), expressing the hero's frustration at what he perceives as contradictory sexual signals on the part of Ylajali. 'What a little devil!' adequately reproduces the sense of this expression. 'By the living Jesus' (p. 175), the choice of Bly, seems utterly out of place. Incidentally, this particular passage is one of the prize exhibits of translators' traps. It begins with the expression, 'Nei men du store min!' (Well, I never!) – translated absurdly as 'Oh, you little fox!' – and contains another preposterous rendering as well, one that smacks of the bizarre, in that the hero's thought, 'Var Piken fra Forstanden?' ('Was the girl out of her mind?'), is given as 'Girl at a distance, beware!'

I shall now look fairly closely at one particular passage of the translation to show how the original text is distorted in essential ways. The limping old man near the beginning of the book is an object of intense interest to the hero/narrator during his morning walk. Since the only source for our knowledge of the old man is the retrospective narrator, any changes to the text affect everything:

the image of the old man, the implicit portrayal of the 'I', the account of what takes place, even the description of the setting.

The old man is from the very outset described in rather grotesque terms. For example, he 'walked with his whole body, struggling with all his might to make headway' (gik med hele sit Legeme, arbeidet av al Magt for at skyte Fart, p. 10).[4] Bly's rendering, 'He ... was using his entire body to move forward, working with all his strength and yet making very little progress' (p. 8), dilutes the sentence and detracts from the physicality of the image, while at the same time attributing an excess of reasoning ('yet making') to the observer. In the next paragraph, the descriptive adjectives 'skrøpelig' (decrepit, sickly) and 'masede' (bustling, flustered) appear as 'feeble' and 'tedious', respectively, characterisations that fail to account for the observer's evident disgust with the man; instead, they would betoken boredom or pity. The immediate visual impression of the old man is subsequently reinforced by the statement that he 'swung his bundle high in the air' (svang Bylten høit i Luften), whereas saying that he 'had taken a stronger hold of his bundle', Bly's rendering, conveys scarcely any visual image. Another detail of observation, subjective in nature, is vitiated by the translator's tendency to reproduce frozen expressions literally: he looked 'determined to make a place for himself in the world *by force and violence*' (med Vold og Magt) instead of '*at all costs*' (my emphasis). This translation undermines one's perception of the very character of the old man: to ascribe to this 'decrepit', 'sickly' creature even the possibility of getting his way by means of 'force and violence' is quite senseless; it represents a kind of gratuitous absurdity that Hamsun scrupulously avoids. The phrase 'at all costs' carries no such inappropriate semantic baggage.

It should be stressed that the 'I' acts throughout in the role of an increasingly emotional observer, one who is so obsessed by the lame man that one begins to suspect an unconscious identification with him. The obsessional quality of his attention is evident from the formulation '*jeg går og ser på* dette masede Væsen', here perhaps best translated as '*I keep watching* this bustling creature' (my emphasis), instead of Bly's incorrect, quasi-literal translation: 'I walked on, looking at this tedious creature'. This type of construction ('gå' + 'og' + another verb) is often the Norwegian counterpart of a continuous tense of the second verb in English. In other ways, too, the Bly translation skews the image of the main character. For example, the hero's annoyance at 'having him [the old man] before . . . [his] eyes all the way' (hele Veien ha ham for mine Øine) is something quite different from fearing 'I would have him blocking my view the whole way', which sounds as though what is important to him is to have an unobstructed view of the cityscape. The 'I' is by now quite agitated and slightly paranoid, a state of mind that obviously slants his observations: 'In my agitation it *seemed to me* that he slowed down a little at every cross street' (my emphasis; I min Ophidselse forekom det mig at han ved hver Tværgate sagtnet en smule). Here again Bly's version, 'I had *become convinced* that . . . he had hesitated . . .', falsifies the psychology of the 'I' by converting a verb implying sensory perception into one with intellectual-cognitive content. The same applies to translating 'jeg følte' as 'it was clear'. Bly's conversion of the past tense into the pluperfect goes hand in hand with this shift, by increasing the sense of retrospective reflection on the part of the hero.

The setting and the physical action are also presented inaccurately in the translation. The narrator may be grandiloquent at times, but there is no reason to translate 'den skjønne Morgen' (the beautiful morning) as 'magnificent morning'. Nor do I see any justification for the inaccurate translation of the following clause: 'jeg vendte mig mot et Butiksvindu og stanset for at gi ham Leilighet til at komme væk' (I turned toward a shop window and stopped to give him a chance to slip away), which in Bly's version becomes 'I stopped in front of a shop window, and waited till he had time to get away'. In fact, this is misleading as well as inaccurate: it sounds as though he actually did 'get away', which is not the case. In the next sentence a categorical statement is changed into a mere assumption: instead of giving the correct rendering, 'he too had stood stock-still' (også han hadde stått bom stille), the translation reads 'he must have stopped also'. Again, it may be noted, observation gives way to reflection. The translation of the last sentence of the paragraph, 'Jeg gjorde . . . tre fire rasende Skridt frem, indhentet ham og slog Manden på Akslen' is true to form: 'rasende' (furious) is rendered as a weak 'quick' and 'slog . . . på Akslen' as the rather chummy 'slapped him on the shoulder', instead of the more appropriate 'tapped him on the shoulder'.

Almost every paragraph of this translation is equally inaccurate, and often grossly misleading. In the passage just discussed, the visual sharpness is diminished, the amount of purely mental activity exaggerated. The image of the lame man is less graphic than in the original, and the hero's psychological disposition is distorted. Compounded over an entire novel, mere approximations of this kind tend to produce a quite different text, as does the translator's conversion of *erlebte Rede* (free indirect discourse) into direct discourse, a tendency that is all-pervasive, and the automatic conversion of the present to the past tense in the general narrative. These falsifications are as serious as the 'howlers' and other verbal mistranslations I have noted above.

The narrativising of dialogue, i.e. presenting dialogue in the form of *erlebte Rede*, is a distinctive facet of Hamsun's fictional style and ought to be respected. Hamsun presents relatively small portions of dialogue in direct discourse; most of it is melded with the narrative. The effect is to create a certain distance from the immediate encounter taking place; the narrator's presence is almost always felt. Hamsun's usage in this respect produces a constant shift in point of view and of narrative distance. Something similar can be said concerning the alternation of the past and the present tense in narration. This, too, entails a play with distance and perspective which a translator should be alive to and attempt to reproduce.

Automobile manufacturers have a long-standing tradition of recalling cars that are defective. We all understand why – there might otherwise occur damage to and loss of human life. It is a pity that publishers do not take potential cultural damage with equal seriousness, damage to the writer's reputation and to all those who are deceived into believing that they have a reasonably reliable text in front of them. The American translation of Hamsun's *Hunger* is definitely due for recall.

It is hoped that future translators of Hamsun will treat his text with the respect it deserves and make an effort to reproduce the nuances of his language as well as the idiosyncrasies of his technique. Only in this way will the English-speaking world be able to read Hamsun's works in a form that does justice to his artistic achievement.

Sverre Lyngstad

NOTES

1 Knut Hamsun, *Hunger*. Translated by George Egerton. New York: Alfred A. Knopf, *c*. 1899.

2 Knut Hamsun, *Hunger*. Translated by Robert Bly. New York: Farrar, Straus and Giroux, *c*. 1967.

3 All citations from the Norwegian text of *Hunger* are taken from Knut Hamsun, *Sult* (Oslo: Gyldendal Norsk Forlag, Hjemmenes Boksamling, 1953).

4 This passage is on pp. 10–11 and pp. 8–9 in the Norwegian and the English text, respectively.

Appendix

SVERRE LYNGSTAD

The comparison of the Bly translation* and the current version is presented in the following way: the first column gives the original Norwegian word or phrase, followed first by the Bly translation and then by the Lyngstad translation.

1. WORDS AND PHRASES THAT ARE 'HYPERBOLIC' IN RELATION TO THE SOURCE TEXT:

HAMSUN	BLY	LYNGSTAD
rynkede Bryn (8)	eyebrows scrunched up (5)	knitted brows (5)
for trist (9)	hopeless (6)	too dreary (5)
tok fat på (9)	plunged immediately into (6)	began (5)
nedslagen (9)	crushed (5)	discouraged (5)
blandet med (9)	into which . . . fit perfectly (6)	mingled with (5)

* *Hunger*, translated by Robert Bly, Farrar Straus Giroux (1967).

HAMSUN	BLY	LYNGSTAD
mere og mere tilfreds (9)	more content and at peace (6)	more and more contented (5)
gnage grådig (13)	chewing savagely (11)	gnawing greedily (9)
hvemsomhelst (14)	any ass (12)	anybody (10)
de Spaserende (14)	the mob (12)	pedestrians (10)
mange (14)	dozens of (12)	many (10)
en mærkelig Retning (15)	a lunatic direction (13)	an odd direction (11)
forvirrede Tilstand (16)	deranged consciousness (14)	confused state (11)
min lille desperate Tiltale (16)	my desperate and petty persecution (15)	my little desperate remark (12)
et Bytte for (16)	a battleground for (15)	at the mercy of (12)
det gir et Ryk i mig (18)	I felt something wrenched in me (16)	feel a jolt (13)
opta (20)	obsess (20)	occupy (16)
nokså (20)	extremely (20)	rather (16)
likefrem (21)	absolutely (20)	simply (17)
gav mig nye Indtryk (22)	obsessed me (23)	gave me new impressions (18)
dessværre (24)	a shame (25)	[he was] sorry to say (21)
gjøre det av med ham (26)	settle his hash (27)	finish him off (22)
Det skal være en flink Mand (26)	They say he's got quite a head on him (27)	He's supposed to be an able man (22)

forsøkende sig frem (26)	pushing forward (27)	feeling his way (22)
Situationen (26)	the plot (27)	the situation (22)
hadde klaret det hele (27)	had settled down marvelously in the job (28)	had managed it all (23)
den gamle Dværg (31)	the little old troll (34)	the old dwarf (27)
Røverkjøp (33)	pure thievery (36)	a bargain (29)
det kunde aldrig falde mig ind (40)	nothing could ever force me (45)	it would never occur to me (37)
gjøre mig til Kjæltring (44)	make a rat of myself (50)	turn myself into a crook (41)
rigtig gruelig leit (45)	a gruesome embarrassment (52)	an awful shame (42)
bet Tænderne sammen (46)	ground my teeth (53)	clenched my teeth (43)
irettesatte (46)	scolded (53)	reprimanded (43)
med Vold og Magt (66)	come hell or high water (79)	by hook or by crook (64)
ta sine Forholdsregler (72)	give me hints to stay away (87)	take his precautions (70)
De må ikke forsnakke Dem (77)	You mustn't make reckless statements (94–95)	Mind your tongue, please (76)
klaget sig (78)	grumbled (95)	complained (77)
av Utmattelse (80)	from exhaustion and fatigue (97)	because of exhaustion (79)
bitterdød (80)	by God and hell (97)	by golly (79)
Streker (80)	idiotic tricks (98)	tricks (79)

HAMSUN	BLY	LYNGSTAD
forrykket fuldstændig alt (81)	completely destroyed everything (98–99)	made a total muddle of everything (80)
kavet imot mig med Hånden (91)	shooed me out with his hands (111)	motioning me off with his hand (90)
kunde ikke se mildere ut (97)	could not have looked more full of milk and honey (119–20)	couldn't look more gentle (97)
Beundring (97)	awe (120)	admiration (97)
gi mig et avslående Svar (97)	get rid of me (120)	give me a refusal (97)
forundrer mig (97)	astounded me (120)	strikes me with wonder (97)
Nøden (102)	hunger and misery (126)	want (102)
Usselhet (110)	infamy (136)	meanness (110)
flau (113)	shocked (140)	embarrassing (114)
før jeg faldt sammen (115)	while I was still in one piece physically (143)	before I broke down (116)
knækket sammen (116)	broken in two (144)	broken-down (117)
forstyrret (118)	delirious (146)	distraught (119)
begyndte at tumle med (118)	became obsessed with (147)	started grappling with (119)
forstokket Sjæl (120)	hardened and damned soul (148)	hardened soul (120)
glædet . . . så det hadde Skikk (120)	given a paradise of joy (148)	made . . . ever so happy (120)
visket ut 123)	whisked away (153)	erased (124)

Ubehag (124)	disgust (154)	discomfort, an uneasy feeling (125)
jeg føler mig råt påvirket (124)	I felt a nausea (154)	I feel rudely affected (125)
kravle mig væk (133)	creep away on my hands and knees (166)	scramble off (134)
Prat (140)	snappy talk (174)	chatter (141)
Skjøgesprog (156)	whore language (193)	gutter language (158)
hvad som interesserte mig hos henne (161)	what was wonderful about her (200)	what interested me about her (164)
men kjære (163)	but, old boy (202)	but dear me (165)
trække av med (164)	make the grade with (204)	walk off with (167)
det adspredte mig (172)	I was fascinated (214)	I found it amusing. (175)

2. EXAMPLES OF STEREOTYPICAL OR FROZEN EXPRESSIONS IN TRANSLATION:

HAMSUN	BLY	LYNGSTAD
kvasse som Kniver (8)	sharp as knife ends (5)	sharp as razors (5)
med Vold og Magt (11)	by force and violence (9)	through brute force (7)
strande (14)	be left high and dry (12)	come to nothing (10)
satte Næsen i Veiret (18)	looked up at the sky (17)	stuck my nose in the air (14)
randt mig ihu (21)	ran through my mind (21)	came back to me (17)

HAMSUN	BLY	LYNGSTAD
jeg kunde dø på (24)	I'd be willing to risk my life (25)	I could bet my life (20)
jeg frøs som en Hund (43)	I was shivering like a dog (49)	I was frozen stiff (40)
lo av fuld Hals (45)	laughed from deep in his chest (52)	roared with laughter (42)
efter alle Kunstens Regler (46)	after the correct rules of the art (54)	according to all the rules of the game (43)
våt som en Hund (61)	wet as a dog (73–74)	wet as a drowned rat (60)
jeg gav det hele en god Dag (83)	I said goodbye to the whole bunch (101)	I didn't give a hoot for them (82)
jeg hadde ligget i Sælen (85)	I had slept in the harness (104)	I had put my shoulder to the wheel (84)
tryglet hen i Hyt og Veir (86)	beseeched the air and the sky (105)	making wild entreaties (85)
sluke . . . med Hud og Hår (96)	swallow . . . bones and all (119)	swallow . . . whole (96)
Navnet skjæmmer ingen (122)	that name is no disgrace (151)	What's in a name anyway? (122)
skamme sig som en Hund (126)	feel no more shame than a dog (156)	cringe with shame (127)
når Ulykken endelig skulde være ute (129)	considering that some catastrophe was clearly looking for me (159–60)	as far as accidents went (130)
nu om Dagen (165)	now during the day (205)	these days (167)
sætter avsted over Stok og Sten (176)	leaped over all obstacles (219)	tear along at full speed (178)

3. EXAMPLES OF EXCESSIVE CONCRETENESS IN BLY'S AMERICAN TRANSLATION:

HAMSUN	BLY	LYNGSTAD
spekulere på en Utvei til litt Frokost (35)	think of some avenue that would lead to breakfast (39)	devise some means of getting breakfast (31)
det forekom mig (35)	I had the sensation (40)	it seemed to me (32)
Lystighet (57)	laughter (68)	merriment (55)
Mørket hadde besat min Tanke (64)	the dark had captured my brain (77)	the darkness had taken possession of my thoughts (62)
brystet var mest betændt (82)	my chest burned the most (99)	my chest was most affected (81)
mit Bryst var i en sørgelig Forfatning (105)	my chest was giving me pain (129)	my chest was in a sorry state (105)
jeg led meget av den [Maten] (110)	my stomach felt upset (135)	it gave me great pain (110)
Bulderet oppe i Rommet (114)	thunder in the sky (140)	the rumble from space (114)
da Gjærningen skete (125)	when he was giving change (155)	when the deed took place (126)
Feberen hadde presset mig ganske voldsomt (127)	my fever had gone up considerably (157)	the fever had been quite rough on me (128)
Ord som store, klamme Udyr (156)	words like huge, cold-blooded reptiles (193)	words . . . like big clammy monsters (158)
som et duknakket Kryp (159)	like a lizard with its head bent to the side (198)	like a humped insect (161)

HAMSUN	BLY	LYNGSTAD
de hadde været tre glade Sjæle sammen (163–64)	we were three lambs out on a spree, that sort of thing (203)	they had been out together, three merry souls (166)

4. EXAMPLES OF REDUCED CONCRETENESS AND SPECIFICITY:

HAMSUN	BLY	LYNGSTAD
iagtta (10)	examine (7)	observe (6)
jeg fik en forunderlig Fornemmelse av (16)	I had a sort of vague conviction (14)	I began to have an odd sensation (12)
lot . . . trænge ind på mig (10)	let . . . influence me (7)	laid myself open to (6)
fornam (18)	recognized (17)	perceived (14)
Gjenvordigheter (20)	setbacks (20)	adversities (16)
hadde i Sinde (21)	had decided (20)	meant, intended (17)
en Ånde mot mit Jeg (23)	a ghost of my 'I' (24)	a breath upon my being (19)
fik i Sinde (24)	decided (25)	took it into my head (20)
jeg følte al min Nysgjærrighet dirre mig gjennem Nerverne (25)	I felt my curiosity become unbearable (27)	I felt my nerves tingling with curiosity (22)
Hehe, det var da Fan! (26)	Amazing! (27)	Hee-hee, I'll be damned! (22)
jeg faldt sammen, blev slap (28)	I returned to normal, became relaxed (31)	I slumped over, grew limp (25)

føler sig frem med lange Tråder (29)	put out expeditions, feeling with their long antennae (32)	grope their way with their long feelers (26)
rynkede Klør (31)	folded claws (34)	wrinkled claws (27)
rapse (36)	steal (40)	snatch (32)
tomme (37)	aimless (42)	empty (34)
hvad Sikkerhet hadde jeg (37)	how did I know (43)	what guarantee did I have (34)
Ørefik (41)	brawl (47)	slapped (38)
rullende Verdener (43)	orbiting universes (49)	whirling worlds (40)
herlig Følelse (44)	magnificent conviction (51)	glorious sensation (41)
underlig slynget Vei (44)	curious paths (51)	strangely winding path (41)
jeg har det så ondt (50)	I have such tribulation (59)	I'm so miserable (47)
gjøre flere Omstendigheter (50)	make any elaborate plans (59)	make any more fuss (48)
Nød (55)	troubles (66)	privation, distress (53)
lidende (55)	afflicted (66)	aching (53)
Nervetrækning (56)	reflex (66)	twitch of the nerves (54)
frådende Herlighet (58)	overwhelming joy (70)	foaming splendour (56)
bitter i Sind (62)	furious (74)	bitter at heart (60)
beskjæftige (64)	bother (77)	absorbed (62)
steilet imot (67)	fought against (80)	recoiled from (65)
skimte (68)	recognize (82)	make out (66)

HAMSUN	BLY	LYNGSTAD
dump træt (73)	tired beyond belief (88–89)	dog-tired (72)
Formaninger (79)	advice (97)	admonitions (78)
det gjør mig vammel av dig (89)	it lowers you considerably in my estimation (109)	it makes me feel disgusted with you (88)
å husere med mig (99)	to take hold in me again (122)	to play havoc with me (99)
Gjenvordigheter (99)	troubles (123)	tribulations (99)
skjælvende (100)	hesitant (124)	trembling (100)
forresten stod det mig frit for (108)	anyway, I still had freedom of action (134)	anyway, it was all up to me (109)
maten begyndte at virke (110)	the food began to bother me (135)	the food began to take effect (110)
fortvilet (114)	confused (141)	desperate (115)
Død og Pine! (118)	Marvellous! (146)	I'll be damned! (119)
slapt (123)	depressed (152)	limply (123)
Motgangen hadde tat Overhånd (124)	circumstances had won (153)	the hardships had got the better of me (124)
besudlet og nedværdiget (124)	lowered in my own estimation, sullied (154)	defiled and degraded (125)
med mørke Miner (129)	and in a hopeless mood (160)	frowning angrily (130)
det voldsomste Sindsoprør (130)	a wild state (162)	a most violent frenzy (131)
plettet Byen (131)	ruined the city (163)	were a blot on the city (132)

tok Mot til mig (135)	did decide to do it (167)	took heart (136)
forsakt (142)	depressed (177)	crestfallen (144)
fortvilet (158)	depressed (197)	desperate (161)
og det gjorde hun sig lystig over (167)	and she made a great deal out of that (208)	and she made merry over it (170)
denne åpenlyse Ondskap (167)	the open enmity (208)	the . . . blatant malice (170)
fik mit Blod til at banke levende (172)	cheered me up (214)	set my heart throbbing (175)
finde på at si (178)	decide (221)	take it into my head to say (181)